Esther

and

Her Elusive God

Esther

and

Her Elusive God

How a Secular Story Functions as Scripture

JOHN ANTHONY DUNNE

With a Foreword by Ronald W. Pierce

WIPF & STOCK · Eugene, Oregon

ESTHER AND HER ELUSIVE GOD
How a Secular Story Functions as Scripture

Wipf & Stock
An Imprint of Wipf and Stock Publishers
199 W. 8th Ave., Suite 3
Eugene, OR 97401

www.wipfandstock.com

ISBN 13: 978-1-62032-784-5

Manufactured in the U.S.A.

For
All the faithful exiles
living in the diaspora of Las Vegas,
a land flowing with filth and money

Contents

Foreword

The biblical book of Esther—that is, the version in the Hebrew Bible recognized as Scripture by Jews and Protestants—has posed a significant challenge to its readers throughout its literary history. Because it makes no mention of God, religion, or theology, it has been embellished, theologized, romanticized, allegorized, heroized—or simply ignored by the church.

In refreshing and insightful contrast, John Dunne takes his readers back to the original version of this most artfully crafted narrative, providing a careful and honest examination of the sacred text as it stands, on its own terms. In doing so, he discovers that Esther is indeed a secular story about an assimilated Jewish remnant in the fifth-century BCE, choosing to live in diaspora after the Babylonian exile in the Persian city of Susa. Esther and her cousin Mordecai show no concern for, or even awareness of, the then-recent restoration of the Jewish people to Jerusalem, or the calling of God to live separate and pure lives before the Gentiles. Dunne concludes that their deliverance in the end is due solely to God's grace and faithfulness to his covenant with Abraham.

My interests in the book of Esther grew alongside my study of the Daniel narratives (esp., chs. 3 & 6). Esther forms a sharp contrast to Daniel and his friends who are rescued *because* they choose to remain faithful to God in exile (see "The Politics of Esther and Mordecai: Courage or Compromise," BBR 2 (1992), 75–89). Also, as an advocate of biblical gender equality, I have been intrigued, and dismayed, at the way Esther is heroized or romanticized by those engaged in the otherwise thanks-worthy task of highlighting the appropriate status and function of godly women in leadership in Scripture. While I continue to applaud their efforts in general, I agree with Dunne that Esther does not fall into this category—a conclusion that has, and will continue to, evoke pushback from many in the church.

The style of *Esther and Her Elusive God* is thoroughly engaging and clear, making it accessible to the non-technical reader without sacrificing academic integrity. Although this is not a traditional commentary, Dunne demonstrates his serious commitment to the inspired and authoritative biblical text, while at the same time interacting thoughtfully and respectfully with the broader world of Esther scholarship. Dunne's unifying themes of the *Comprise, Covenant* and *Cover-Up* (chapters 1–3) make his case for the meaning and message of Esther. The canonical and theological reflections in the *Canon* and *Church* sections (chapters 4–5) address Esther's practical significance for those today that cherish this book as sacred Scripture.

Everyone loves a good story! This creative and insightful contribution by John Dunne has brought one of our favorite stories to us again, yet with a renewed appreciation for its authenticity and the role of biblical narrative. His book is a must-read for anyone that has puzzled over Esther's story—or simply loves it.

Ronald W. Pierce, Biola University
Co-editor, *Discovering Biblical Equality* (2005)
Author, *Partners in Marriage and Ministry* (2011)
Author, *Daniel,* Teach the Text Commentary (2014)

Preface

My interest in Esther began during my studies at Talbot School of Theology where I did an arranged course with Dr. Thomas J. Finley comparing the Greek and Hebrew versions of Esther. Although my current doctoral research under Professor N. T. Wright at the University of St Andrews has focused my attention squarely on the Apostle Paul, and his letter to the Galatians in particular, I have maintained an on-going love for the book of Esther. The present book is the culmination of that original study at Talbot.

I decided to turn that research into a book because I wanted to provide the church with an alternative to the popular understanding of the story, an understanding that I found to be much more in line with the later Greek translations of the story than the original Hebrew. My aim was to provide a balance between a broadly accessible book for generally interested readers, and something intended for an academically inclined audience. For this reason I have chosen to interact with an eclectic array of sources on Esther, from the scholarly monographs and journal articles to the more lay-focused devotions and commentaries, and even the popular retellings of the story in romance novels, films, and cartoons.

Writing this book in the summer of 2013 while in the midst of a PhD program was challenging in many ways, not least because of the temporal and cultural gulf between Galatians and Esther. Yet despite how disparate the two biblical books appear, there is a unifying theme that connects my research on the two books—persecution. My research on Galatians focuses on Paul's faithful response to persecution and suffering, and his desire for his audience to imitate him as he follows the crucified Messiah.[1] Of course,

1. See my "Suffering in Vain: A Study of the Interpretation of ΠΑΣΧΩ in Galatians 3.4," *Journal for the Study of the New Testament* 36.1 (2013): 3–16; *idem*, "Cast Out The Aggressive Agitators (Gl 4:29–30): Suffering, Identity, and the Ethics of Expulsion in Paul's Mission to the Galatians," in *Sensitivity to Outsiders: Exploring the Dynamic Relationship between Mission and Ethics in the New Testament and Early Christianity*, ed. Jacobus Kok, Tobias Nicklas, Dieter Roth, and Christopher M. Hays (WUNT II; Tübingen: Mohr Siebeck, *forthcoming* 2014); *idem*, "Suffering and Covenantal Hope in Galatians:

the story of Esther is about how the Jews were able to thwart a systematic pogrom directed against themselves. The context of persecution provides an interesting link, but in the case of Esther we do not see a faithful response to persecution (as I argue in this book). The sort of response to persecution that I think Paul expected of his readers is sadly the opposite of what takes place in Esther.

Unless otherwise noted, I have used the NIV translation throughout this book. For a few biblical citations I chose to use the NRSV, yet those places are clearly marked and my choice of the NRSV is explained. For citations of the "Apocrypha," including the Additions to Esther, I used the NRSV.

At this point a number of thanks are in order. I want to begin by thanking Dr. Ronald W. Pierce for his interest in this book, for providing feedback on the full manuscript, and for writing the Foreword. I also wish to thank those who read portions of my previous drafts, such as, Rev. Paul Clarke, Samuel Emadi, Diamond Patrick, Sean Thomas, and Prof. Kristin De Troyer, as well as those who read through the entire manuscript, including, Brad Blakeley, Ernest Clark Jr., Kevin Collier, Tim Fox, Gerald Lofquist, Bryan Magaña, and Calvin Sodestrom. Special thanks are due to fellow colleagues in St Mary's College who participated in an informal discussion night on Esther after reading through the full manuscript. These are Garrick Allen, Penny Barter, Isaac Blois, Chris Brewer, Jen Gilbertson, Christina Larsen, and Jesse Nickel. I am incredibly grateful for the willingness of each person listed above. Their feedback, written notes, corrections, encouragement, and criticism helped move the book forward into its present shape.

Finally, I dedicate this book to the faithful exiles in Las Vegas. I have in mind all the godly men and women I have had the privilege of meeting while growing up in "Sin City," those who live everyday trying to make sense of Jesus's distinction between being in the world but not of the world (John 17:6–19). Among these I can think of no greater examples than my own parents, John and Nancy, who have worked in the Casino business for over forty years between the two of them, and yet demonstrate such consistent faithfulness to God, showing me what the people of God should look like if they find themselves in a pagan king's palace.

John Anthony Dunne
All Saints' Day, 2013

A Critique of the 'Apocalyptic Reading' and Its Proponents," *Scottish Journal of Theology*, forthcoming.

Introduction

We may ignore, but we can nowhere evade, the presence of God.
The world is crowded with Him. He walks everywhere *incognito*.[1]

—C. S. LEWIS

The tension expressed in the quote above by C. S. Lewis, between the hiddenness of God and his nearness, was central to his theological reflection. This emphasis was no doubt related to his concerns as a literary critic, especially his interest in what he called "the kappa element" of stories.[2] This element "has to remain hidden," as Michael Ward describes, yet it is "woven into the warp and woof of the story."[3] Michael Ward himself demonstrated just how committed Lewis was to embedding hidden elements within stories by showing how each of the seven books in *The Chronicles of Narnia* corresponds to one of the seven heavenly bodies within medieval cosmology. This fascination with God's hiddenness and nearness, absence and immanence, propelled Lewis's theological, fictional, apologetic, and literary career.

It is through a similar lens that many understand the elusive God of Esther. God remains hidden in the story, never mentioned of course, but many believe his presence is implied, assumed, suggested, or (paradoxically) emphasized on every page.[4] Yet does such an approach really do justice to the story?

1. Lewis, *Prayer: Letters to Malcolm*, 272 (emphasis original).

2. From Lewis's essay "The Kappa Element in Romance," addressed to Merton College in November of 1940, which was then updated and retitled as "On Stories."

3. Ward, *Planet Narnia*, 18.

4. As an example of this, Berlin (*Esther*, 44) states regarding the fourth chapter of Esther, "God is most present and most absent in this chapter."

Perhaps you have heard sermons or participated in Bible studies on Esther. Or you might even recall Sunday school lessons about Esther from when you were a child. It may also be the case that you have seen the many cartoon and film versions of Esther, such as:

- *Esther and the King* (1960)
- *Exile: Esther* (1986)
- *The Greatest Adventure: Stories from the Bible; Queen Esther* (1992)
- *Animated Stories from the Bible: Esther* (1993)
- *The Bible: Esther* (1999)
- *VeggieTales: Esther, the Girl Who Became Queen* (2000)
- *One Night with the King* (2006)
- *Esther and the King: Musical Adventures in Faith* (2010)
- *The Book of Esther* (2013)

Or, just maybe—no judgment I promise—you have read one of the many Esther-inspired romance novels (if I passed judgment you could point out the log in my own eye!). Some notable examples include:

- *Esther*, by Norah Lofts
- *A Reluctant Queen: The Love Story of Esther*, by Joan Wolf
- *Esther the Queen*, by Heather B. Moore
- *Esther: The Star and Sceptre*, by Gini Andrews

Doubtless many have engaged the story countless times, in multiple venues and platforms, and have found great inspiration from it.

There are several reasons to be interested in Esther, especially since it is one of the most unique books in the entire Bible.[5] Esther is one of only two biblical books to be named after a female (the other is Ruth). It is also the only book in the Bible to depict activities that take place exclusively outside of the land of Israel. The book of Esther explains the origin of the Feast of Purim, which is the only biblical festival not found in the Torah. Additionally, the book contains the single longest verse in the entire Bible (see Esth 8:9), including over eighty words in the majority of English translations. Most shockingly, though, the book of Esther does not have a single reference to God.[6] We do not find the personal name YHWH, titles or other

---

5. When I refer to the Bible I have in mind the sixty-six books of the Protestant canon.

6. It may also be the only book in the Bible like this depending on the interpretation/translation of Song of Songs 8:6. See further comments on p. 27.

divine names, such as Adonai, Elohim, or El-Shaddai, nor are there any pronouns that have God as their referent. In addition to this, the story does not include any of the typical religious vocabulary that we might expect; there are no references to prayer, repentance, worship, or faith, nor do we find any particularly Jewish aspects of religion, such as references to the covenants, the temple, the promised land, the Sabbath, the law of Moses, circumcision, purity, righteousness, godliness, holiness, or dietary laws. These omissions are ultimately because, as I hope to show, *Esther is a secular story*. That is to say, *secular* in the sense that the people of God portrayed in Esther appear to have experienced a decline in faith and religious adherence to the God of their ancestors; an effect due ultimately to the result of *assimilation*, the undoing of Israel's commission to be "set apart" from the nations.

But the important thing to mention here is that the Esther story does offer evidence that *the author* was aware of biblical history, biblical phrases, and biblical concepts. This means that we as interpreters need to figure out *how* the author utilized these biblical aspects. The tension between Esther as both *biblical* and *secular* is at the heart of this book and will be addressed throughout. What we will find is that the author of Esther was a very sophisticated and subtle writer. Note the confession made by a senior Jewish scholar, Jon Levenson:

> For the author of this commentary affirms without reservation that a few years of close textual work on the book and involvement in scholarship on it have immeasurably enriched his reading of it and proven it in his mind to be a vastly more complex piece of literature than he had previously thought.[7]

In agreement with this assessment, I regard Esther to be the chief narrative of the Old Testament in terms of literary skill, story-telling, and subtlety. The story is gripping, intriguing, humorous, ironic, and delightfully ambiguous. The starting point of this study, therefore, is the assumption that Esther is a misunderstood story.

The Aim of the Present Study

My primary interest is in the Hebrew text of Esther preserved for us in the medieval Masoretic Text (MT); the text that Protestants claim as canonical

---

7. Levenson, *Esther*, 1.

and inspired, and which many Evangelicals also call inerrant. Besides the Hebrew text, another version of the story is also considered to be a sacred text by Catholics and the Orthodox. This version is rooted in a Greek translation of Esther dating from the second or first century BCE and comprises part of what has come to be known as the Septuagint (LXX). This Greek version, and other ancient expansions, will be addressed at various points, but our main focus is the original Hebrew version of Esther. Sadly, most Protestants and Evangelicals do not appropriately engage the Hebrew version found in their Bibles. Esther is either *neglected* by those who claim that its words are significant, or, if not neglected, is *adjusted* in such a way that significantly distorts the story. These adjustments, ironically, have much more in common with the Greek version of Esther than the Hebrew. Those of us who are Protestants should seek to correct this by preserving and maintaining the Hebrew version of Esther as valuable for Christians and the church on its own terms. This book is therefore a call for those who claim to embrace the Hebrew version of the Esther story to genuinely do so.

The lack of any reference to God, the absence of religious vocabulary, and the relative dearth of anything specifically Jewish within Esther are surely the most perplexing issues of the story. All too often these omissions are themselves omitted from consideration; readers tend to import God, religion, theology, piety, and devotion *into* the text. This can be seen in many popular studies on Esther, the films, the children's cartoons, and the romance novels. In fact, this phenomenon began with the earliest known interpretations of the story.[8] Whether in ancient or contemporary expressions, this process of importing theological and religious imagery does not do justice to how the story was originally intended to be read and understood. So instead of trying to fill in the divine blank, as is so often done, we should recognize that the author's avoidance of religion and theology was entirely deliberate and intentional. Through various literary devices, such as allusion to antecedent Jewish Scriptures and the use of irony, we can see how the deliberate omission of religion and theology was intended. I will argue that the missing pieces ultimately point in one direction—toward the secularity and assimilation of God's people.[9] And yet, this unfaithful people experienced such an incredible deliverance—attended by multiple

---

8. E.g., the two Greek translations of Esther (the Septuagint [LXX] and the Alpha Text [AT]), Josephus's retelling in his *Antiquities*, the two Aramaic translations (known as Targums), the interpretation of Esther in the Babylonian Talmud, etc.

9. So also Pierce, "Politics of Esther," 75–89; Huey, "Esther," 787.

"coincidences"—that we will ultimately be led to conclude that the elusive God of Esther was steadfast and faithful, preserving his people though they did not deserve it.

Background Issues

If you pick up any commentary on Esther—or practically any other book of the Bible for that matter—there is a basic script that commentators typically follow. It is customary to begin by addressing the basic starting points and presuppositions that color many of the conclusions drawn within the commentary proper. These questions include authorship, dating, genre, intended audience, provenance, and more. This book, however, is not technically a commentary on Esther, and so there is very little need to labor these points at length. For the purposes of this book I will only make a few brief comments since the conclusions do not affect the nature of this study.

Dating

Esther was most likely written sometime between the death of King Xerxes I (465 BCE) and the collapse of the Persian Empire to the Greeks (331 BCE). The three main reasons for this perspective are (1) Esther 9:19 implies that the Festival of Purim had become an established tradition with the passing of time, (2) the Hebrew vocabulary shows little influence from the Greek language, and (3) the book as a whole conveys a remarkable acquaintance with Persian culture and custom.[10] For these three reasons, and others, it is perhaps safest to conclude that the book was written by an anonymous Jew sometime in the late Persian period or early Hellenistic period.[11]

Genre

Because some aspects of the book are thought to be fantastical or exaggerated, such as the use of numbers—the height of the gallows being seventy-five cubits; the destruction of 75,810 Persians in two days of battle; the reference to 127 provinces within the Persian Empire; the 180 day feast;

10. So Waltke and Yu, *Old Testament Theology*, 765.

11. So Jobes, *Esther*, 28–30. For a Hellenistic setting, see Fox, *Character and Ideology*, 139–40.

and the one-year beauty pageant—and because of historical oddities, such as the lack of any evidence for a queen named Vashti in Persian history, let alone a Jewish queen named Esther, the historicity of Esther has been called into question.[12] Some of these peculiarities could correspond to an accident of archeology, that is to say, we may not currently have evidence but such could surface in the future with further archeological research.

On the other hand, the alleged problems with historicity must be evaluated in relation to the genre of Esther. Was the book intended to be historical? Several scholars have suggested that Esther is not strictly a history but a *story*. Esther has been called, among other things, (a) "a divinely inspired short story,"[13] (b) a "historicized wisdom-tale,"[14] (c) "a comic story for a carnivalesque holiday"[15] that is "a burlesque of historiography,"[16] and (d) a "historical novella set within the Persian empire."[17] It should not be assumed, however, that "story" for these authors necessarily equates with falsehood. As Jon Levenson explains, "This is not to say that the book is false, only that its truth, like the truth of any piece of literature, is relative to its genre, and the genre of Esther is not that of the historical annal."[18] Even the beloved C. S. Lewis regarded Esther to be a "story," but this would not have devalued the text in any way for him. Commenting in a personal letter about biblical books like Jonah, Job, and Esther, he stated that these are examples which show that the Bible includes, in addition to sacred history, both sacred fiction and sacred myth, as well.[19]

Some scholars have actually made cases for the historicity of the story, such as Edwin Yamauchi.[20] Though most take a middle position and argue, like Carey Moore, for a historical core, calling Esther a "historical

---

12. Fox, *Character and Ideology*, 131–39; Paton, *Critical and Exegetical Commentary*, 64–77.

13. Goldingay, *Ezra, Nehemiah, and Esther*, 7.

14. Talmon, "'Wisdom' in the Book of Esther," 426.

15. Berlin, *Esther*, xvi.

16. Ibid., xxviii.

17. Levenson, *Esther*, 25.

18. Ibid., 25.

19. See the letter to Janet Wise on 5 October 1955, in Lewis, *Collected Letters*, 652–53. See also the letter to Corbin Scott Carnell on 5 April 1953, in Lewis, *Collected Letters*, 318–19.

20. Yamauchi, *Persia and the Bible*, 226–39. Also, for archeology of Susa, see Yamauchi, *Persia and the Bible*, 279–303, and for historical background of Xerxes I, see Yamauchi, *Persia and the Bible*, 187–226.

novel."[21] Whatever we make of Esther's genre, if Esther was not intended to be historical then we have no reason to regard the alleged discrepancies as a blight on the author's historical skills. For example, does the historical probability of Jesus' parables impact their effectiveness, meaning, or intent? Stories are not to be held to the same scrutiny as history. Related to this, it is also the case that our post-Enlightenment conception of history needs to be held in check when we think about how ancient historians conceived of historicity. It may very well be the case that Esther is both history and story, and at the very least, if it is history, it is history mediated through a well-crafted story.[22] Ultimately, deciding whether or not Esther was written as history or story is beyond the scope of this brief introduction. We will therefore proceed to evaluate the Hebrew text in its final form and on its own terms. Before proceeding it may be worthwhile to provide an overview of that tale.

Overview of the Book of Esther

As a way of providing a reference to the story of Esther, I have written the following summary. You are invited to read the story for yourself in preparation for this book and to turn back at various points along the way.

The story begins with Ahasuerus[23] on the throne in Susa as the king of the Persian Empire. Immediately we learn that this king would apparently rather party and show off his opulence than do anything else; after hosting a dinner party lasting 180 days he quickly proceeds to entertain a seven-day banquet. On the seventh day of this banquet the king "was in high spirits from wine" (1:10)—which is no doubt bound to take place when you party harder than someone pledging to join a fraternity for over six months—and he summoned his wife, Queen Vashti, to appear at his banquet to display

---

21. C. Moore, *Esther*, xxxiv–liii.

22. See similar comments in Jobes, *Esther*, 30–37.

23. The name of the king in the Hebrew text is "Ahasuerus" (see "Artaxerxes" in the LXX). This is most likely a Hebraized form of the name of the Persian king (better known by his Greek name Xerxes I), who ruled from 485 to 465 BCE. To avoid confusion for those utilizing various translations of Esther in conjunction with this book—since one may find the king's name to be translated as either "Ahasuerus" (so KJV; NKJV; ESV; NASB; NRSV; HCSB; NET) or "Xerxes" (so NIV; NLT)—I have chosen to refer to this figure simply as "the king" in most instances. However, Xerxes I is certainly the historical referent (as opposed to Artaxerxes I). For Ahasuerus as Xerxes I, see Paton, *Critical and Exegetical Commentary*, 51–54.

her beauty. Vashti, who was hosting her own banquet for the women, refused the "invitation." This made the king furious and so he summoned his courtiers for advice. It was decided that Vashti should be sent away lest women throughout the empire become insubordinate to their husbands.

Eventually the king felt the need to replace Vashti. Again, the courtiers devised a plan for the king; it was determined that virgins should be brought to Susa, given beauty treatments, and then brought before the king. Whoever pleased the king would be the one to replace Vashti. The virgins were all given one night with the king to make their impression. One of these young women was a Jewish orphan girl named Hadassah who was raised by her cousin Mordecai. Hadassah, who we know as Esther, was forbidden by Mordecai to reveal her "family background and heritage" (2:10). Of all the women brought before the king, it was Esther who delighted him the most. She was given the crown and became the replacement of Vashti. As a celebration of this occasion, the king hosted a banquet—again!—and "distributed gifts with royal liberality" (2:18).

Sometime after this, Mordecai uncovered a plot to kill the king, and the would-be assassins, Bigthana and Teresh, were sentenced to death. Mordecai's loyalty to the king was recorded in the king's chronicles, but oddly enough he was never rewarded for this deed. Instead, it was announced that Haman—"the Agagite"—had been promoted and thus all those of inferior rank were required to bow before him in reverence. All but Mordecai showed Haman the deference that was due; Mordecai refused and said it was because he was a Jew that he disobeyed. This made Haman furious; he determined that Mordecai should pay for his defiance, and not just Mordecai alone, but the rest of his people, as well. Haman cast *pur*, or lots, to decide what day the Jews were to be destroyed. The lot fell on the thirteenth of Adar, the last month of the year, but at this point it was only the thirteenth of Nisan, the first month, so the destruction of the Jews would have to wait a while. Nevertheless, Haman swiftly presented this proposal to the king in a rather sly manner, speaking obliquely about "a certain people" that separated themselves and kept their own laws instead of the king's (3:8). Upon hearing this, the king agreed to exterminate them. An edict was written, sealed with the king's signet ring, and sent to all the provinces.

The news quickly spread and many Jews throughout the provinces, including Mordecai, clothed themselves in sackcloth and wept bitterly. Mordecai was able to communicate with Esther while she was in the royal palace through the mediation of Hathach, one of the king's eunuchs, and informed her of the edict. Mordecai realized that the only hope for the survival of the Jews was if Esther went before the king and begged on behalf of her people. After Esther showed initial hesitancy—because anyone who appeared before the king un-summoned would be sentenced to death—Mordecai convinced her that she would not survive the edict if she did not go to the king, since she was also a Jew. So Esther resolved to go—*damned if I do, damned if I don't*—and called for the Jews to conduct a three-day fast along with her before she went to the king. "And if I perish," she said, "I perish."

After the third day, Esther donned her royal robes and went before the king. Instead of facing the wrath of the king, however, Esther was welcomed and offered anything she would like, "up to half the kingdom" (5:3). Esther responded by inviting the king and Haman to a banquet she prepared for them.[24] During the banquet the king tried to discern what Esther's request was, and she asked for the two of them to return again for another banquet the following day. Haman left the banquet quite pleased with himself for having been invited to two private banquets with the king and queen, but on his way home he walked past Mordecai who once more refused to show any deference to him. This infuriated Haman, and after complaining to his wife and friends, they decided to build a pole[25] in their yard to impale Mordecai the following morning; the thirteenth of Adar could not come soon enough.

However, that very night the king was unable to sleep and so he summoned a courtier to read from the historical annals of his reign. The courtier *just happened* to read about the plot that Mordecai had thwarted which saved the king's life. Curiously, there was no mention of any reward given to Mordecai for his loyalty. So while the king was thinking of how to honor Mordecai, Haman *just happened* to be entering the court with the intention of speaking to the king (since he was coming to request that Mordecai be impaled). Once Haman entered, the king asked him what should be done

24. The Hebrew literally reads that the banquet was "for him." It is unclear whether it refers to the king or to Haman. Most commentators assume that the reference is to the king, or that somehow both Haman and the king are meant by the singular pronoun. For a defense of the position that the banquet was meant for Haman, see McClure, "Esther's Banquet for Haman."

25. In conjunction with the NIV, the translation used throughout this book, I refrain from using the anachronistic term "gallows" here and elsewhere. In Persian society, criminals were not hung, as in a Western movie, but impaled.

for the person that the king wished to honor. With an air of unmatched presumption, Haman assumed that the king *must* have been referring to himself and so he suggested an elaborate display of honor involving a parade with a royal steed and royal attire. The king loved the idea and demanded that nothing be left out, except that Haman was to do this *for Mordecai*. So instead of impaling Mordecai, Haman paraded him around town in regal fashion. As we might expect, Haman returned home humiliated, and his wife Zeresh admitted that this downfall would continue to spiral out of control because Mordecai was a Jew (6:13). Then in the midst of his frustration and humiliation, the courtiers of the king arrived to announce that the banquet was ready.

At the second banquet that Esther prepared for the king and Haman, the king asked again what Esther's request was. This time Esther begged for her life and the life of her people, telling the king that Haman's edict was meant for the Jews. The king left the room in fury and while he was outside Haman pleaded to Esther for his life. Upon returning to the room, the king accused Haman of making a sexual advance on his wife and sentenced him to death on the very pole meant to impale Mordecai.

In the aftermath, Mordecai was promoted and received the king's signet ring as well as the estate of Haman. However, the edict against the Jews was still in full force and could not be revoked (8:9). So another decree was written that essentially reversed the edict of Haman. On the thirteenth of Adar the Jews would be permitted to assemble and kill anyone who attacked them. This led to great rejoicing on the part of the Jews throughout the entire empire and likewise led many Gentiles to join the side of the Jews (8:17).[26] Fear of the Jews spread throughout the empire, and when the thirteenth of Adar came the Jews destroyed their enemies, including the ten sons of Haman, ostensibly without even suffering a single casualty. After the day's fighting was over, Esther requested another day of fighting in Susa and that the ten dead sons of Haman be impaled (9:13). Thus, in Susa there were two days of fighting, leaving 810 people dead, and throughout the provinces there was only one day of fighting, leaving 75,000 people dead. The two days of fighting in Susa, instead of the single day of fighting elsewhere, is given as the explanation for why rural Jews celebrate the fourteenth of Adar as a day of feasting whereas the urban Jews celebrate on the fifteenth in the continual observance of Purim (9:16–32). Esther and Mordecai wrote letters to all the Jews in the provinces calling them

26. I address the meaning of this verse on pp. 60–61 of chapter 2.

to continually celebrate Purim as an annual festival commemorating their deliverance. The story ends with a final note about Mordecai's promotion to second in rank behind the king.

With the story of Esther now fresh in our minds we are ready to dive into the main arguments of this book. Before we do so, here is a quick road map for what is ahead.

Overview of Esther and Her Elusive God

Unlike a commentary, this book will not comment on every verse of Esther. Likewise, this book will not proceed in a perfectly sequential fashion from the first chapter of Esther until the conclusion. Rather, this study will progress in a thematic outline. Essentially this book seeks to answer the following question: *How does this seemingly secular story function as Scripture?* Thus, the manner in which I have arranged the material attempts to answer that question according to the flow of thought that seems most natural to me. It is hoped that my readers will agree.

The first half of the book contains three chapters addressing issues of interpretation within the text of Esther (part 1) where the primary concern is to determine how we should read the story of Esther on its own terms before considering the canonical and theological implications this has for the church in the final two chapters that form part 2.

The first chapter (*Esther & the Compromise*) tries to demonstrate that, rather than being exemplars of faith, Mordecai and Esther are quite impious and show a strong amount of assimilation to their pagan context. The focus of this chapter is primarily Esther 2.

In the second chapter (*Esther & the Covenant*) I focus primarily on Esther 3–4 and 8–9, addressing the question of whether or not there could be some religious imagery that shows the characters might have had a sense of faith, piety, and devotion. I argue that there are no positive examples in this regard, corresponding to the manner in which the first chapter (*Esther & the Compromise*) showed evidence of impiety. Chapters 1–2 together then build the cumulative case for the assimilation and secularity of the characters.

Despite the intentions of the author to avoid religious and distinctly Jewish vocabulary from the story, some the earliest known interpreters of it—the Greek translator(s) of the Septuagint (LXX) and Alpha Text (AT), and the Aramaic translator(s) of the Targums—felt the need to insert significant additions to make the theological and spiritual message of the story explicit. Thus, in chapter 3 (*Esther & the Cover-Up*) I address the possibility that these translators were attempting to "convert" the text, so to speak. Those readers that are particularly interested in the complex set of issues raised in this chapter will want to consult the appendix for further argumentation. This chapter also analyzes the popular versions of the Esther story and seeks to demonstrate that their retellings follow the same trajectory as the early Greek and Aramaic translations. Collectively the three chapters of part 1 corroborate the claim that the characters in the Esther story were secular and assimilated. Both the text of Esther (chapters 1–2) and the way that text was altered (chapter 3) demonstrate this.

After considering issues of interpretation in part 1, part 2 explores some canonical and theological reflections. In the light of the case made throughout the first three chapters of this study, chapter 4 (*Esther & the Canon*) addresses the question: *Does Esther belong in the canon of Christian Scripture?* If we are to give a positive answer, we are then left immediately with another vexing question: *How exactly does the book of Esther fit in the canon?* This then leads directly into the fifth and final chapter (*Esther & the Church*), where I attempt to articulate the theological message of this difficult book, lest we assume that the text of Esther really does not belong in the Bible after all. In considering precisely how the Hebrew story of Esther fits within the canon of Scripture, I will point out how to place Esther in canonical concert with the message of the Bible. This final chapter will therefore act as a suitable conclusion to our study.

I hope you will enjoy engaging the story of Esther with me.

Part One

A Secular Story

1

Esther & the Compromise

The typical interpretation of the Esther narrative is perhaps familiar to most. The story depicts the courage of a young woman who was able to save her people despite the odds. The general perception regarding the key protagonists, Esther and Mordecai, seems to be that they were exemplars of faith and virtue in the midst of these tumultuous events. Yet in this chapter I will try to demonstrate that the version of Esther that we are used to does not do justice to the original story. Our aim, therefore, should be to reconsider the evidence, and to determine whether it is the case that Esther and Mordecai were exemplary models of devotion and piety. What I will argue is precisely the opposite; there appears to be evidence that the protagonists were unfaithful to the God of their ancestors. Thus, this chapter will attempt to unravel the popular conception of Esther and Mordecai by looking at the examples of compromise. In the following chapter (*Esther & the Covenant*) it will be argued that the typical instances in the story where many find examples of devotion do not actually support such readings. Together these first two chapters provide a cumulative case for the secular and assimilated nature of the Jewish characters in the story.

At first glance it may seem unfounded to have a chapter on "compromise" in the book of Esther. The author never says explicitly that anyone had sinned against God or had broken any law from the Torah. So we are left to wonder what the perspective of the author actually is. Lest we think that the author's avoidance of making judgments in the narrative implies complete approval, we ought to remember that he also never tells us things that most readers intuitively assume, such as, the opulence of the king's feasting in chapter 1 was excessive and indulgent, or that Haman's desire to kill all the Jews was evil. The reader is not privy to such evaluation. Are we to assume that, because the Jews were ultimately the victors at the end of the story, our author finds all the actions of the Jews favorable or, at the least, justifiable? Are we to assume further that the moral lines in the story are clearly drawn, that there are good characters on one side and bad characters on the other? This is actually a difficult question for the whole of the Old Testament. How many Old Testament narratives have such clear demarcations between completely good characters and completely bad? Such narrative characterization would turn characters into caricatures and be quite unrealistic.

We must acknowledge however that the author's reticence to inform his readers of his explicit evaluation of the story is not a sign of his indifference to the situations he depicts. Nor could it be inferred that since the author does not explicitly chide the characters in any way that he must condone their behavior (this is manifestly false in the case of Haman). Rather, the story of Esther is told in such a way that the motivations, desires, and intentions of the characters are kept secret. Note Joyce Baldwin's assessment, "As compared with modern story-telling this presentation is entirely objective; the author avoids comment, attempts no character study, no psychological interpretation, passes no judgment. The reader is left to make his own deductions."[1]

This narrative characteristic of Esther is fairly consistent with other portions of the Old Testament where the narrator refrains from commenting on the morality of certain situations. For instance, in Genesis 19:30–38, Lot's two daughters decided to carry on their family line through sleeping with their father. After getting him drunk on consecutive nights they took turns sleeping with him and both of them conceived. As the text reads, there is no assessment of their actions; nothing is said to be "abominable in the eyes of the Lord" or anything like that. The author presumably refrained because he believed that the story would be perceived a certain way on its own terms.

Part of the problem here is that readers of the Bible all too often assume that they should be basically sympathetic to the main characters of a biblical narrative. One needs only to look at the story of Judges to recognize that this is not an appropriate assumption. Additionally, such assumptions may cause the reader to misinterpret individual sequences within broader narratives, such as Abraham giving his wife Sarah away as his "sister" twice

1. Baldwin, *Esther*, 63.

(Gen 12:10–20; 20:1–18), and Isaac doing the same with Rebekah (Gen 26:1–11). In fact, a whole narrative could be misread in the example of Jonah. If we read that story with the intent of sympathizing with his actions, we will entirely miss the author's point. The author of Jonah does not want readers to accept Jonah's position as valid, or to be sympathetic to his concerns. Of course, the author of Jonah never says these things explicitly but this is communicated through the events in the story, as well as the use of humor and irony. Thus, when we consider the story of Esther we need to try to be in tune with how our author, and other Jews of his time, would have interpreted various actions within the story.

In this chapter the focus will primarily be on Esther 2:1–18. Ultimately, we will see that the typical view of Esther and Mordecai fails to account for a number of important factors, which we will explore in further detail below. The first is the background of the exile. Of course, we all know that the story of Esther is the story of a young Jewish woman who becomes the queen *of Persia*. But we need to stop and reflect on *why* the story takes place in Persia, outside the land of Israel. The second issue is the list of figures associated with Esther and Mordecai (Esth 2:5–6) that raise immediate red flags about the characters—a sort of "guilty by association" connotation. The third issue is the fact that Esther and Mordecai are actually pagan Babylonian names. Finally, there appears to be many misunderstandings about the nature of Esther's involvement in the so-called "beauty pageant" designed to choose a replacement for Queen Vashti. This evidence, as we will see, leads us toward the conclusions of other scholars who have stated that "there is not one noble character in this book,"[2] and that "the main characters of the book are scarcely models of virtue or piety."[3]

The Effects of Exile

Exile & Diaspora

One thing that readers of Esther often miss is that the sin of the Jewish people looms over the book of Esther from the very beginning. The story takes place outside the land of Israel in Susa where the king of Persia reigns over the world. In the midst of this pagan kingdom we are introduced to a Jew named Mordecai (2:5). *But what is he doing so far away from the land*

2. Paton, *Critical and Exegetical Commentary*, 96.

3. B. Anderson, "Place of the Book of Esther," 38.

of Israel? He found himself in this foreign land as the result of the exile (2:6), which came about as the punishment for Israel's sin. Just as Israel had conquered the indigenous peoples living within the promised land in accordance with God's promise (Gen 12:6–7), so Israel was likewise uprooted from the land. The reason for this was because the law of Moses had promised Israel blessings for obedience to the law and curses for disobedience, the chief of which was exile (Deut 28:36–68). The northern tribes of Israel were overtaken by Assyria in the late eighth century BCE (2 Kgs 15:29; 16:9; 17:5–23; 18:9–12), and the southern tribes of Judah were captured by Babylon in the early sixth century BCE (2 Kgs 20:16–18; 21:10–15; 23:27; 24:1–4; 1 Chr 9:1). It is this latter Babylonian captivity that sets the context for our story.

At the time that Babylon overtook Judah they also sacked Jerusalem, destroyed the temple, and plundered it (2 Chr 36:6–7; Jer 52:17–23; Dan 1:2; 5:2). Yet Babylon was later overthrown by the Persians (Jer 50–51) who succeeded them as the next major world power. A decree from the Persian king, Cyrus the Great, announced that the Jews could return to their land (2 Chr 36:22–23; Ezra 1:1–4; 7:3–12; Isa 44:28; 45:13), that the sacred vessels which Babylon had stolen from the Jerusalem temple were to be given back (Ezra 1:7–11; 5:13–15), and that the Jews could rebuild the temple (Ezra 6:15). However, some Jews did not return to Jerusalem, including Esther and Mordecai. The decree from Cyrus was made before the setting for the story of Esther; thus the Jews in Susa were not compelled to be there. So why did they not return to Jerusalem? Furthermore, why do we not read about their concern to be where the temple of God was, to be where the people of God were, or to be in the land that God had promised them? What makes this more intriguing is the fact that Susa is in the opposite direction from Jerusalem, even further away than Babylon.

What we see in the Esther story, then, is not "exile" properly speaking, but rather *diaspora*. The distinction between exile and diaspora offered by Jo Carruthers is worth citing here:

> I use "exile" to signify a dispersed community in which identity is centered on a homeland, and "diaspora" to indicate a coherent yet non-territorial identity recognized by other characteristics such as religion or race.[4]

---

4. Carruthers, *Esther through the Centuries*, 33.

However, this transition of perception, shifting the land of exile into diaspora, is itself a negative product of exile. The lack of a desire for the homeland should be seen as part of the assimilation that took place during the exile. That such a reorientation is indeed a negative result of the exile can be seen in the prophet Jeremiah's desire that the exilic community "remember the lord in a distant land, and call to mind Jerusalem" (Jer 51:50). The same desire is reflected in the words of the psalmist:

> If I forget you, Jerusalem,
> may my right hand forget its skill.
> May my tongue cling to the roof of my mouth
> if I do not remember you,
> if I do not consider Jerusalem my highest joy. (Ps 137:5–6)

Thus, when we look at the story of Esther and see the apparent indifference of the Jews toward Jerusalem, the temple, and the land of Israel, it appears to be a glaring omission.

In addition to this impact of the exile, the list of names in Esther 2:5–6 also provides intriguing background from which to evaluate the context of exile in the story. The first are the ancestors listed in the genealogy of Mordecai in 2:5, Kish and Shimei, and the second is King Jehoiachin in 2:6. We will look at each in turn.

A Negative Genealogy: Kish and Shimei

When Mordecai is first introduced in 2:5 the reader learns that he is the descendant of two figures from Israel's history, Kish and Shimei. Perhaps these figures do not immediately pop out as important biblical characters, but here we see some of the author's subtlety; these figures are lesser-known relatives of King Saul. This oblique reference to Saul, despite its subtlety, is vital to understanding the conflict between Mordecai and Haman "the Agagite" (see 1 Sam 15). We will consider the importance of Mordecai and Esther's heritage to King Saul for the conflict with Haman in more detail in the next chapter, but for now it is important to recognize the effect of Mordecai's introduction as it reflects on the context of exile.

Mordecai is said to be a descendant of Kish (Esth 2:5), who was the father of Saul (1 Sam 9:1–2; 1 Chr 8:33; 9:39; 26:28). What we see then in this link to Saul is an intentional correspondence between Esther and Saul as regal figures, and the correspondence goes beyond royalty. Just as Saul was a very attractive person, being "as handsome a young man as could be found anywhere in Israel" (1 Sam 9:2), so too Esther was exceedingly beautiful (Esth 2:7). However, the connection to Saul is not a positive one. Although Saul was the first king of Israel, the very act of making him king was seen as part of Israel's rejection of God—"they have rejected me as their king" (1 Sam 8:7). Additionally, Saul was a disobedient king, being rebuked by Samuel for not keeping the Lord's commands (1 Sam 13:1–14). In fact, the assessment of Saul's life as a whole is quite negative—"Saul died because he was unfaithful to the LORD" (1 Chr 10:13). The prophet Hosea even proclaimed sharp words regarding the appointment of Saul—"So in my anger I gave you a king, and in my wrath I took him away" (Hos 13:11). The connection to Saul therefore shows that although Esther and Mordecai had regality in their blood, it was *bad* regality.

Mordecai is also introduced as a descendant of Shimei (Esth 2:5), who was a relative of Saul (2 Sam 16:5; 1 Kgs 4:18). Once again, this reflects a negative lineage. Shimei is known as the one who cursed David and pelted him with stones (2 Sam 16:6–7, 13). David responded to this curse by saying, "It may be that the Lord will look upon my misery and restore to me his covenant blessing instead of his curse today" (2 Sam 16:12). Some time later Shimei fell prostrate before David and begged for mercy, calling what he did "sinful" (2 Sam 19:18–20), and David let him live (2 Sam 19:21–23). Although when David handed the kingdom over to Solomon, the very last thing David said before he died was that Shimei should be put to death for cursing him and the kingdom (1 Kgs 2:8–9). In the exchange of power, the final thing that Solomon did before "the kingdom was established" under his reign (1 Kgs 2:46) was have Shimei executed (1 Kgs 2:36–46). Thus, it is highly ironic that Mordecai, a descendant of Shimei, was living in the aftermath of the curse upon the nation of Israel that led to the downfall of David's kingdom. In fact, we are told that Mordecai was led into exile along with Jehoiachin (Esth 2:6),[5] one of the very last kings of Judah before the Babylonian exile, and himself a descendant of David.

A Negative Association: Jehoiachin

Jehoiachin was king in Jerusalem for only three months before he was taken away to Babylon by Nebuchadnezzar (2 Kgs 24:8, 12). Yet for those

---

5. I do not think that Mordecai and Jehoiachin were contemporaries; rather, I assume that the text expresses corporate solidarity in exile.

three months he was a wicked king (2 Kgs 24:9). After 2 Kings describes the destruction of the temple in Jerusalem, it concludes with a scene where Jehoiachin is released from prison and elevated to a high status; for the rest of his life he ate at the Babylonian king's table (2 Kgs 25:27–30). The scene is brief and no commentary is provided. It is often suggested, though, that 2 Kings ends this way as "a note of hope,"[6] showing a glimpse of the end of exile. Even if Jehoiachin was meant to embody a positive glimpse of the end of exile—and this is likely the case—it is still also likely that Jehoiachin's release was not the result of God showing him favor for some sort of obedience. For one, we do not read about him repenting anywhere. Second, the only comment we receive about Jehoiachin's behavior is that he did what was wicked in the eyes of the Lord (2 Kgs 24:9; see also 2 Chr 36:9). And last, the book ends with Jehoiachin eating regularly at the king's table (2 Kgs 25:29). Since 2 Kings is the last book within a collection of books commonly known as the "Deuteronomistic history" (i.e., Joshua, Judges, 1–2 Samuel, 1–2 Kings)—called such because of the keen interest of these authors in telling Israel's story through the lens of Deuteronomy and its stipulations regarding covenant blessings for obedience and covenant curses for disobedience—it is therefore highly unlikely that these historians, who emphasized adherence to the law, would have looked upon Jehoiachin eating pagan food positively. The "Deuteronomistic history" begins with the promised land gained (the conquest in Joshua), and ends with the promised land lost (Babylonian captivity in 2 Kings). Thus, the Deuteronomistic historians had a particular theodicy in mind as they retold their history—*how did we end up in exile?* The answer is expressed through their theological interpretation of events; obedience to the law leads to blessings, disobedience leads to curses. It seems very unlikely, therefore, that these historians would have held a positive view of Jehoiachin, even if they saw in him a reason to be hopeful. For these reasons it is preferable to regard Jehoiachin's release in 2 Kings as ambiguous, conveying both the imminent end of exile as well as showing the unworthiness of Israel for experiencing such deliverance.

The Lord declared through the prophet Jeremiah that even if Jehoiachin was a signet ring he would still be cast off into exile (Jer 22:24–27); the implication being that he is not like a signet ring. Further, Jeremiah prophesied that none of his offspring will prosper and none from his lineage will sit on the throne of David to rule over Judah (Jer 22:28–30). From

---

6. So Waltke and Yu, *Old Testament Theology*, 737.

Jeremiah's vision of two fig baskets—one good, one bad—we do learn that those initially taken to Babylon comprise the good basket of figs (Jer 24). This, of course, has nothing to do with their behavior—otherwise they would not be going off to exile!—but rather signifies that the initial group of exiles have hope for a return and a future relationship with the Lord when they receive from him "a heart to know me" (Jer 24:5–7). Intriguingly, Jeremiah ends the same way that 2 Kings does—with an ambiguous depiction of Jehoiachin eating at the Babylonian king's table (Jer 52:31–34).

The biblical evidence seems to indicate that Jehoiachin was not an exemplary figure, and even if his release was deemed a sign of hope, it nevertheless remained problematic. So the association of Mordecai and Esther with Saul (by implication), Shimei, and Jehoiachin, casts a negative light on our characters in the exile. Furthermore, evidence of assimilation even extends to the very names *Esther* and *Mordecai*.

The Babylonian Names

In one of the Esther-inspired romance novels written for a Mormon (LDS) audience, *Esther the Queen*, Haman is depicted as reacting negatively to hearing the name "Mordecai"—"Just the sound of the Jewish man's name caused Haman to shudder because it was so . . . Jewish."[7] Well actually . . . it is not; it is Babylonian.

The name "Mordecai" comes from the name of the Babylonian god Marduk and literally means "man of Marduk" or "worshipper of Marduk."[8] Additionally, Esther appears to be named after the Babylonian goddess of love and war, Ishtar. Both characters also show a remarkable similarity to their namesakes who are the chief god and goddess of Babylon respectively. The Babylonian cosmogony and theogony, The Epic of Creation (*Enuma Elish*), records how Marduk ascended to the top of the Babylonian pantheon, and the story of Esther records a similar ascension for Mordecai within the Persian rank (see Esth 10:1–3).[9] For Esther, her association with

---

7. H. Moore, *Esther the Queen*, 172.

8. Jobes, *Esther*, 96; Yamauchi, *Persia and the Bible*, 234.

9. For other key texts regarding Marduk, see the following (in Hallo and Younger, *Context of Scripture*): *Erra and Ishum* (COS 1.113), *Prayer to Marduk* (COS 1.114), *Weidner Chronicle* (COS 1.138), *Marduk Prophecy* (COS 1.149), *Sufferer's Salvation* (COS 1.152), *Poem of the Righteous Sufferer* (COS 1.153), *Cyrus Cylinder* (COS 2.124), *Laws of Hammurabi* (COS 2.131).

Ishtar is likewise apparent—like the goddess of love Esther wins the king's "beauty pageant" to become queen and like the goddess of war she oversees the military victory at the end of the story that leads to a sizeable body count of the enemies and ostensibly zero casualties for the Jews.[10] These comparisons are remarkable, and when it is recognized that the deities Marduk and Ishtar are cousins, just as Mordecai and Esther are cousins, the comparisons are unmistakable.[11]

According to Elias Bickerman, the pagan names point to the possibility that the story is really an amalgam of two originally unrelated narratives from pagan sources that became united—"Whatever was the origin of the two tales we have tried to reconstruct, in Jewish folklore the hero and the heroine naturally became Jewish."[12] This could then be an explanation for the lack of religious significance of the story. But why would the characters be made Jewish without really resembling Jews in any obvious way? We might assume that if the story was indeed originally a Babylonian tale, or something along those lines, that the story would have been transformed into a polemical rewrite of the Babylonian tale filled with explicit Jewish expansions. The lack of Jewish revision seems to debunk this argument.

Some try to explain away the correspondence between Esther and Mordecai with Babylonian deities by appealing to the story of Daniel. A few popular retellings of Esther make this precise connection.[13] For instance, in the film *One Night with the King*, when Esther is about to be taken to the

---

10. In the Epic of Gilgamesh, Ishtar's role as the goddess of love is shown when she tries to entice the hero (and elsewhere). For other texts on Ishtar, see the following (in *Context of Scripture*): *Ritual and Prayer to Ishtar of Nineveh* (COS 1.65), *Descent of Ishtar to the Underworld* (COS 1.108), *Nergal and Ereshkigal* (COS 1.109), *Erra and Ishum* (COS 1.113), *Diurnal Prayers of Diviners* (COS 1.116), *Etana* (COS 1.131), *Laws of Hammurabi* (COS 2.131). For Inanna, the Sumerian version of Ishtar, see esp. *Exaltation of Inanna* (COS 1.160), *Inanna and Enki* (COS 1.161), *Dumuzi-Inanna Songs* (COS 1.169A-C), and *Sacred Marriage of Iddin-Dagan and Inanna* (COS 1.173).

11. As noted in Paton, *Critical and Exegetical Commentary*, 88–89. Esther's name could be polyvalent, meaning "star" in its Persian context (Fox, *Character and Ideology*, 30) and "hidden" in its Hebrew context (from the verb *str*) as well (Allen and Laniak, *Ezra, Nehemiah, Esther*, 206). Although these possible meanings are relevant to the story, especially Esther's "hidden" nature (see 2:10, 20), the connection to Ishtar appears to be in the forefront.

12. Bickerman, *Four Strange Books*, 186.

13. The popular versions also undermine the significance of our protagonists bearing pagan/Babylonian names by introducing additional Jewish characters to the story with stereotypically Jewish/biblical names (e.g., Dan, David, Jacob, Jesse, Judith, Leah, Rachel, Rebekah, Sarah, Shimeon, etc.).

king's palace she is told by Mordecai that her name should no longer be "Hadassah," but "Esther," and likewise, her childhood friend Jesse, who was captured and made into a eunuch, was given the name "Hathach" (one of the actual eunuchs in the story; see Esth 4). When they finally reunite in the king's palace, Esther specifically claims that the experience of Daniel's three friends is analogous to theirs. In Gini Andrews's novel *Esther: The Star and the Sceptre*, Esther is given the name "Esther" only after arriving at the king's palace.[14] In this novel the correspondence to Daniel is more direct since Esther had her name changed by the pagans. In fact, in this story she is quite reluctant to use her new name.[15]

Of course, Daniel and his three friends (Hananiah, Mishael, and Azariah) had their names changed to Belteshazzar, Shadrach, Meshach, and Abednego, respectively. Yet there are two problems with finding an analogy between Esther and Daniel along these lines. The first problem is that these characters, especially Daniel, are not always referred to in the narrative by their pagan names after the name change (see Dan 1:11, 19; 2:17 for Daniel's friends).[16] However, the opposite is the case with Esther and Mordecai. We know of no other name for Mordecai, and, although Esther has a Jewish name ("Hadassah"), it is only mentioned once. The second problem is that the pagan names were forced upon Daniel and his three friends, whereas there is no indication along these lines in Esther.

Karen Jobes contends that if the names of Esther and Mordecai are to be connected to the Babylonian deities, "the outcome of the story suggests to the Babylonian pagans that Marduk and Ishtar are subservient to the purposes of the unnamed God of the Jews. The victory of the Jews in this story would then function as a polemic against the pagan deities."[17] Yet how this functions as a polemic is uncertain since it is *Esther and Mordecai who are victorious in the story.* Jobes's perspective places the emphasis of critique upon the pagan deities being represented, when really it appears to be intended the other way around, as a critique of those *representing* the deities. The Babylonian names call into question in what sense these characters are "Jewish" even though Mordecai is often referred to by the appellation, "Mordecai the Jew." For Michael Fox this shows that Mordecai is an ideal and representative Jew who is a man identified first and foremost

---

14. Andrews, *Esther*, 86.

15. Ibid., 90.

16. See also Gen 41:45 when Joseph's name was changed to "Zaphenath-Paneah."

17. Jobes, *Esther*, 97.

and finally by his Jewishness."[18] Yet there seems to be a note of irony in the appellation because Mordecai is a lowest common denominator sort of Jew in the story of Esther. His heritage is purely and solely ethnic for him, and this is how the cognate terms are utilized in the story. Where do we find any *religious associations* that make Mordecai "Jewish"? Furthermore, we must not fail to recognize the assimilation inherent in the appellation "*Mordecai the Jew.*" I suggest that these pagan names ultimately point to the assimilation of the characters who bear them. And being Babylonian names they point to the assimilation that took place as the result of exile.

Foreign Marriage

One of the main areas of disobedience that led to the exile was foreign marriage. This draws our attention to the infamous "competition" that Esther was involved in to replace Vashti, and ultimately won. As Ronald Pierce rightly notes, "Esther's marriage to Ahasuerus tragically mimics one of the key failures of the Jewish people that resulted in her family being brought to Susa."[19] This link between foreign marriage and the exile is expressed quite forcibly in Joshua's farewell address after the conquest of the land:

> But if you turn away and ally yourselves with the survivors of these nations that remain among you and if you intermarry with them and associate with them, *then you may be sure that the lord your God will no longer drive out these nations before you.* Instead, they will become snares and traps for you, whips on your backs and thorns in your eyes, *until you perish from this good land,* which the lord your God has given you. (Josh 23:12–13; emphasis mine)

The implication of Joshua's speech is that exile was one of the consequences of intermarriage (see Josh 23:15–16).

In the patriarchal narratives of Genesis we see a strong aversion to mixed marriage as well. Rebekah said her "life will not be worth living" if Jacob married a Hittite (Gen 27:46). Isaac commanded Jacob not to marry a Canaanite woman (Gen 28:1), and when Esau heard of Isaac's prohibition (Gen 28:6) he intentionally disobeyed since his father found it so displeasing (Gen 28:8–9). Shechem wanted to intermarry with Jacob's children, swapping daughters for daughters after he raped Dinah (Gen 34:9, 21),

---

18. Fox, *Character and Ideology*, 186.

19. Pierce, "Politics of Esther and Mordecai," 84.

but Jacob's sons refused, killing Shechem and the men of his city (Gen 34:25–29).

The problem with foreign marriage in the Old Testament is that it fosters idolatrous tendencies. Moses warned that if foreign women are taken as wives Israel will be led to "prostitute themselves" to foreign gods (Exod 34:16). When Israelite men began to engage in sexual activity with Moabite women they started making sacrifices to other gods (Num 25:1–3; see also 31:16), and it is in this context that we read of Phinehas's zeal in killing an Israelite man and Moabite woman during a sexually promiscuous act (Num 25:6–9). The Lord warned against intermarriage because foreigners "will turn your children away from following me to serve other gods" (Deut 7:3–4). In Judges, an exchange of daughters in marriage between the Israelites and foreigners resulted in serving other gods (Judg 3:6). Likewise when Ahab married the Gentile Jezebel this led to Baal worship and other forms of idolatry (1 Kgs 16:31–33). Malachi wrote that Judah desecrated the temple through intermarriage (Mal 2:11); the reason for this was because these women "worship a foreign god." The indictment here in Malachi is quite strong: "As for the man who does this, whoever he may be, may the LORD remove him from the tents of Jacob—even though he brings an offering to the LORD Almighty" (Mal 2:12). Malachi may be echoing the words of Deuteronomy as well—"No one born of a forbidden marriage nor any of their descendants may enter the assembly of the LORD, not even in the tenth generation" (Deut 23:2).

There are, of course, examples of mixed marriages that are not problematic at all. For instance, the marriage of Boaz to a Moabite woman named Ruth was appropriate given the fact that she embraced Israel's God (Ruth 1:16; 2:12). Expressing the general sensibilities against mixed marriages, Miriam and Aaron found it odd that Moses married a Cushite woman (Num 12:1 see also Exod 2:21), yet Moses was vindicated in this instance because, again, the problem was not with mixed marriages *per se*, but only the propensity toward idolatry. Samson married a Philistine woman, and although his parents did not support the idea—no doubt because of sensibilities consistent with the laws of their people—the narrator notes that the Lord was using this marriage as a military strategy (Judg 14:3–4). In the light of this scene, we may be tempted to interpret Esther's marriage to the king of Persia similarly. Yet to interpret Esther's pagan marriage as a strategy fails to keep in step with the narrative of Esther itself. There was no hostility toward the Jews prior to Mordecai's refusal to bow to Haman in

Esther 3:1–6. And in the case of Samson, the marriage ended about a week after it started (see Judg 14:10–20). Joseph married Asenath, the daughter of the priest of On (Gen 41:45), yet the text does not comment on whether this was good or bad. Later Jewish interpreters felt the need to fill in this love story and describe in vivid detail how this Egyptian woman became a "new creation" when she became a follower of the God of Israel (see *Joseph and Asenath*). We are not told in Genesis if Asenath embraced Joseph's God or not, but we must keep in mind that mixed marriage was not unlawful if it did not lead to a neglect of God. A similar situation can be found in Song of Songs, which is devoted to the love that Solomon shared with a Shulamite woman (Song 6:13). There is a contested reference in Song of Songs 8:6 to the divine name "Yah," which could be short for Yahweh. The Hebrew word in question (*šalheḇetyāh*) would then be rendered as "the flame of Yah."[20] If this is a reference to God, since it is uttered by the Shulamite woman, we can assume an association with Israel's God on her part. But regardless, the problem with foreign marriage was not foreign marriage *per se*, but whether one remained faithful to Israel's God or not.

This marriage to the Shulamite was not the last word on Solomon and mixed marriage, however. Ultimately, this did lead to his own personal downfall, and had corporate effects as well. After Solomon married Pharaoh's daughter (1 Kgs 7:8) as well as other foreign women, we are told:

> King Solomon, however, loved many foreign wives besides Pharaoh's daughter—Moabites, Ammonites, Edomites, Sidonians and Hittites. They were from nations about which the lord had told the Israelites, "You must not intermarry with them, because they will surely turn your hearts after their gods." Nevertheless, Solomon held fast to them in love. (1 Kgs 11:1–2)

To make this issue even more egregious, Solomon is recorded as having seven hundred wives and three hundred concubines! These women led him astray (1 Kgs 11:3) and turned his heart away from the Lord toward other gods, bringing him to the point of even building shrines and altars for these other deities (1 Kgs 11:4–8). So the kingdom was torn apart because of his actions (1 Kgs 11:11–13, 31–33). This would cause a ripple effect that ultimately led to exile.

After the exile, Ezra came to Jerusalem from Babylon sometime after the reign of Xerxes I (i.e., "Ahasuerus") during the reign of "Artaxerxes"

---

20. The NIV renders this word "a mighty flame," yet offers an alternative reading in a footnote, "like the very flame of the LORD."

(Ezra 7:1, 8).[21] When Ezra arrived he heard about the extensive intermarriage that had taken place and how the leaders of Israel "led the way in this unfaithfulness" (Ezra 9:1–2). His response was drastic; he tore his clothes and ripped hair out from his head and his beard (9:3). Then Ezra prayed and recalled how similar sins led to their experiences in exile (Ezra 9:7, 13). He recalled God's command—"Therefore, do not give your daughters in marriage to their sons or take their daughters for your sons" (Ezra 9:12)—and bemoaned the fact that even though God preserved a remnant from out of the exile, the remnant was just as disobedient in engaging in mixed marriages (Ezra 9:14–15). The people responded by weeping and confessing their sin to God (Ezra 10:2). Then Ezra called the people to separate from their foreign wives (Ezra 10:10–11; see also 10:3–4).

We read of a similar response from Ezra's contemporary, Nehemiah, who originally lived in Susa (1:1) and was the cupbearer to King Artaxerxes (1:11).[22] When Nehemiah heard about the destroyed walls of Jerusalem he wept (1:3–4), and went to Jerusalem to help rebuild. After Ezra read from the Law, the people confessed their sins—the sins that led to the exile and the sins during exile—by declaring, "In all that has happened to us, you have remained righteous, you have acted faithfully, while we acted wickedly" (Neh 9:33). The people then made an agreement to follow the Lord's commands and declared, "We promise not to give our daughters in marriage to the peoples around us or take their daughters for our sons" (Neh 10:30). When Nehemiah saw men from Judah with foreign wives (Neh 13:23–24), he rebuked them, called down curses on them, beat them, pulled out their hair, and made them take this oath—"You are not to give your daughters in marriage to their sons, nor are you to take their daughters in marriage for your sons or for yourselves" (Neh 13:25). Nehemiah then reminded them of Solomon's downfall through foreign marriage and rebuked them for carrying out the same wickedness and unfaithfulness (Neh 13:26–27).

So when we put Esther's marriage to the king of Persia in biblical perspective it does not seem to be reconcilable. Are there any hints in the text that might lead us to believe that Esther had good intentions or that our author was completely sympathetic with her? Did Esther want to become queen or was this situation forced upon her?

21. Whether this refers to Artaxerxes I or Artaxerxes II is not clear. See Goldingay, *Ezra, Nehemiah, and Esther*, 4–5, 53.

22. Ezra and Nehemiah are examples of Jews living at the end of the exile in the diaspora (Babylon and Susa) who did not experience assimilation like so many others, including Esther and Mordecai.

Taken Forcibly? Esther 2:8

In Esther 2:8 we read that "Esther also was taken to the king's palace." Some point to the use of the word "taken" as a sign that Esther did not go willingly and that she was a victim in this sequence. Of course, it was determined that *all* virgins throughout the provinces must appear before the king. The so-called competition to replace Vashti was not an optional "beauty pageant" for which contestants could sign up. The king had given a decree.

However, to interpret the word "taken" as "taken by force" is surely misguided. Several reasons suggest this. The first is stylistic. The story of Esther frequently utilizes passive forms of verbs and other passive constructions in its story-telling.[23] For instance, when the Jews assembled to fight on the thirteenth of Adar, the Hebrew literally reads that they were "gathered" (9:2).[24] Of course, this does not mean that they were gathered forcibly at all. The NIV simply renders the beginning of 9:2 with the active sense of "the Jews assembled." Other instances of this could be noted, but the point is that the author's literary consistency in using passive constructions should be considered when making judgments about the force behind the language of Esther being "taken."

Second, rendering "taken" as "forcibly taken" does not do justice to the particular Hebrew verb being used in Esther 2:8. The verb used here (Hebrew: *lqḥ*) is the same verb used twice in the book of Ruth to designate Boaz *taking* Ruth as his wife (Ruth 4:13) and Naomi *taking* their child Obed to care for him (Ruth 4:16). The verb simply does not carry the connotations of force. There are, however, clear examples of rape and forced sex in the Old Testament, such as the rape of Dinah (Gen 34), the concubine of a Levite (Judg 19:25), and Tamar (2 Sam 13); and these scenes are depicted very differently from what we read in the story of Esther. In fact, there is a clear example of the forceful taking of wives in the book of Judges when, somewhat ironically, some Benjaminites forcibly acquired wives (Judg 21:21–23; it is ironic because Esther and Mordecai were Benjaminites). These people "caught" (Hebrew: *ḥṭp*) and "snatched" (Hebrew: *gzl*) women to be their wives. The terms used are completely different and are much more forceful in nature. And none of these forceful sequences bear any resemblance to the scene we have here in Esther.

---

23. So rightly Berlin, *Esther*, xxvi.
24. The verb *qhl* is in the *Niphal* stem (i.e. *niqhălû*).

Third, the sense of "taken by force" misconstrues the desires of the people in the story of Esther. As Michael Fox notes, "We are probably importing a foreign notion if we imagine the maidens would have had to be forced into the harem, for life in the palace would seem desirable to most people."[25] He notes further, "However degrading we may find such herding of women for royal use, the connection with royalty was perceived as a step up in the world for them; it was no small thing to be queen of the Persian empire."[26]

Fourth, and finally, if Esther was taken forcibly, where was the protest? From Esther 4:1–3 we see that Mordecai was more than willing to protest, even in non-subversive ways, and to express his emotions about negative situations. We do not see anything close to this in Esther 2, however, from either Mordecai or Esther. Where was the mourning? The sackcloth? The torn clothes? There was none; apparently they were not bothered by the decree. There was a complete lack of protest and inner-turmoil, and this is telling.

Therefore, the notion of Esther being taken forcibly appears unfounded.[27] It is one thing to read the story of Esther in our twenty-first-century Western and postcolonial setting where the rights of women are emphasized and cherished, and therefore critique the political and cultural system depicted in the story of Esther—and this is all fine and well—but it is another thing to ask how an ancient author who lived within that system, knew nothing but that system, and did not offer a critique of that system, would have considered the events. We are reading a story from a fifth- or fourth-century (BCE) Jewish person in the aftermath of the exile, a period when the covenantal hopes of yesteryear had been decimated by the Babylonians, but now a new era was dawning and some had begun to draw clear lines in the sand. Nationalism was emerging, as seen in the writings of Ezra and Nehemiah, and it was in this milieu that our author wrote, and the initial audience engaged the story. Thus, the notion of foreign marriage would not have sat well with Esther's earliest readers. But if we can safely conclude that Esther was not captured or taken forcibly to the king's palace, what do we know about her intentions? Was she trying to win the competition?

25. Fox, *Character and Ideology*, 33.

26. Ibid., 34.

27. Jobes (*Esther*, 98–99) concludes rightly that it is "probably overinterpreting [*sic*] the passive voice" to interpret this verb as "taken forcibly." Likewise, C. Moore (*Esther*, 21) notes there is no indication that Esther was taken by coercion or that she went reluctantly. See also Paton, *Critical and Exegetical Commentary*, 173.

Hidden Identity & Hidden Intentions

When Esther was about to go before the king as part of the competition, she did not take anything with her beyond what was suggested by Hegai the eunuch (Esth 2:15). Some suggest that this points to Esther's basic modesty.[28] It has also been suggested that this abstinence should be seen as a reticence to engage in the heathen world as in the story of Daniel.[29] However, this could actually be a sign of shrewdness. That is to say, Esther shrewdly took what Hegai, a courtier of the king, thought she should bring to impress. She could have refused to take anything altogether, and in this way tried harder to ensure that she would not win the king's affection. Yet she shrewdly embraced Hegai's recommendations.

We are also told that Esther won the favor of Hegai (2:9), all those who saw her in the harem (2:15), and ultimately the king (2:17).[30] This has been understood as a sign that God was granting her favor in this difficult situation. Beth Moore states that Esther used her "God-driven, Scripture-quickened people skills" to gain favor.[31] David Firth suggests that the reason why Esther gained favor is because she "has made God's priorities her own."[32] But is there anything in the text that even hints at Esther doing such things? In similar situations as Esther, we also read of Daniel and Joseph's experiences of receiving favor in foreign lands. Yet there is an intriguing difference between Joseph and Daniel "finding favor" in a passive sense, and Esther "taking favor" in an active sense.[33] When Joseph and Daniel "find favor" we are also told that it was God who granted the favor (Gen 39:3–4, 21; Dan 1:9). The notion of being granted favor as a result of their obedience is also expressed; in the case of Joseph he had refused to sleep with Potiphar's wife (Gen 39:6–21) and as for Daniel, he had refused to eat the king's royal food while in exile (Dan 1:8). In regards to Esther we are not told that God was blessing Esther's obedience with "favor." Instead, it appears that Esther was seeking favor with the intent to win the competition.

28. Berlin, *Esther*, 28; McConville, *Ezra, Nehemiah, and Esther*, 162; Swindoll, *Esther*, 48.

29. So Fox, *Character and Ideology*, 37.

30. The Hebrew terms used are *ḥesed* (2:9) and *ḥēn* (2:15) and then both together in 2:17. As we will see, the theological usage of these terms elsewhere in the Old Testament should not be imported into this context.

31. B. Moore, *Esther*, 41.

32. Firth, *Message of Esther*, 53.

33. So Bush, *Ruth, Esther*, 368.

After winning Hegai's favor, Esther was given some food (2:9). This raises the issue of dietary laws that would have been problematic for pious Jews. With a story that includes so much feasting and revelry, this issue is thrown in the reader's face over and over again.[34] The food here in 2:9 is not disclosed, but since it is linked to cosmetics it was likely part of the beautification process for the competition.

And what exactly did this competition involve? After the extensive beauty treatments (Esth 2:12), each of the women, one by one, would get an opportunity to go to the king for a night to try to win his favor. The text of Esther 2:14 is implicit but the point is clear—one of the main factors of this competition was sexual performance. Ultimately, Esther was the most successful and became queen (2:17–18).

Is it possible that in breaking the ancestral laws of her people Esther had good intentions? Along these lines we must consider why Mordecai told Esther to keep her Jewish identity a secret (2:10, 20). The concealment of Esther's identity is often interpreted as a means of mitigating conflict. Larson and Dahlen contend similarly, "Mordecai probably wanted to protect Esther from possible anti-Jewish sentiments, the type he experienced from Haman."[35] Carol Bechtel writes that Mordecai must have thought that Esther's "Jewishness puts her at some risk."[36] Likewise Karen Jobes states, "This suggests that Mordecai counseled Esther to conceal her Jewish identity because he had good reason to fear that anti-Semitism was lurking close at hand."[37] Others express this general thought as well.[38]

The problem with interpreting Esther's concealment of her identity as a means of thwarting hostility is that Haman is not introduced until 3:1—which takes place after the year-long competition and after Esther was crowned queen—and we do not find any hostility against the Jews prior to 3:6. Additionally, the events take place in a time period in which Persia was more or less tolerant of other religions and customs, including those of the Jews. Cyrus the Great, as noted earlier, had allowed the Jews to return to

No hostility toward Jews (handwritten margin note)

34. There are ten feasts total, see p. 118 in chapter 5.

35. Larson and Dahlen, *Ezra, Nehemiah, Esther*, 297.

36. Bechtel, *Esther*, 31.

37. Jobes, *Esther*, 99.

38. E.g., Firth, *Message of Esther*, 62; B. Moore, *Esther*, 44; McGee, *Ruth and Esther*, 246; Fuerst, *Books of Ruth, Esther*, 53; Fox, *Character and Ideology*, 32; idem, *Redaction of the Books of Esther*, 113; Goldingay, *Ezra, Nehemiah, and Esther*, 168. We will also see this displayed in both the ancient translations of Esther as well as the modern retellings on pp. 89–90 of chapter 3.

Jerusalem and rebuild the temple. He even returned all the sacred vessels plundered from the temple. So there is no reason to assume that hostility was lurking, or that Esther specifically consented to enter the competition on behalf of her people. If she concealed her identity with the intent of winning the competition[39]—as perhaps another example of shrewdness on Esther's part along with taking only what Hegai suggested and attempting to gain the favor of others—it was not to save her people.

However, I think we are given an important clue about Mordecai's command for Esther to keep her identity a secret from 2:20, when we are told for the second time that Esther concealed her identity. Note the additional comment made in this second reference:

> But Esther had kept secret her family background and nationality just as Mordecai told her to do, for she continued to follow Mordecai's instructions *as she had done when he was bringing her up.* (Esth 2:20; emphasis mine)

So we are told that Esther was following Mordecai's instructions as she always had. However, I think the NIV translation is a little misleading here (see also NLT; HCSB). The word translated as "instructions" is singular in the Hebrew (*maʾămar*; see KJV; NKJV) and is best taken as a reference to *the specific command being referenced*, namely, the command to keep her identity a secret.[40] What this conveys, then, is that the clause "as she had done when he was bringing her up" informs us that Esther had been in the habit of concealing her identity long before this competition.[41] We are not told why, but in this foreign land after the exile we can assume that Mordecai had tried to maintain a sense of normalcy in his foreign context—which is ultimately another sign of assimilation, something we have seen throughout this chapter.

Conclusion & Summary

From this study of Esther 2 it is concluded that Esther and Mordecai were not the paragons of religious piety that many have assumed. Perhaps for

39. So Huey, "Esther," 806.

40. The ESV, NASB, NET, RSV, and NRSV each obscure the singular referent implied by the singular "command" in their translations without inserting the pluralized form of "command" (or synonyms) directly. Cf. the "command" of 1:15 and 9:32.

41. This coheres with the polyvalence of Esther's name, meaning "hidden" in Hebrew (from the verb *str*). See Allen and Laniak, *Ezra, Nehemiah, Esther*, 206.

some of these reasons we can be less surprised that we do not find Esther and Mordecai listed with other exemplars in the famous "Hall of Faith" found in Hebrews 11.[42] At best, Esther's presence in the king's competition is "morally ambiguous."[43] At worst, Esther 2 depicts the great degree to which God's people had become assimilated. What we are left with, ultimately, are the effects of exile. As Kuyper rightly noted, "[Esther] serves to illustrate how far Israel had denigrated while in exile."[44]

It can also hardly escape notice that Esther's participation in a competition to replace Vashti *marks an intentional contrast with Vashti*. Note Barry Webb's comments in regards to Vashti: "Her stout refusal to be used by Ahasuerus has a heroic quality that we instinctively recognize, and this makes Esther's compliance, in what is in many ways a comparable situation, highly questionable."[45] The point of this comparison is not to show how one woman acquiesced to patriarchy and the other defied it,[46] as if critiquing the societal structures related to gender was the intent of the story of Esther. The point is the contrast between *a Gentile and a Jew*. It was ultimately a Gentile woman who was able to defy the king, whereas Esther did not, and in so doing broke several Jewish laws and customs in the process.

Although the author appears to have a laissez-faire attitude in his storytelling, it is hard to imagine that post-exilic Jews would not have quibbled with the story. Perhaps there may be evidence elsewhere in the narrative where Esther and Mordecai demonstrate their commitment to their religious traditions? Perhaps along these lines we may find a "turning point" in the narrative, such as a moment of repentance, that puts the negativity of Esther 2 in a better light? These are the sorts of questions that will be addressed in the next chapter.

42. One cannot even find Esther and Mordecai in the similar list of exemplars found in *Sirach* 44–50 (a pre-Christian "apocryphal" text).

43. Jobes, *Esther*, 114.

44. Kuyper, *Women of the Old Testament*, 174.

45. Webb, *Five Festal Garments*, 120. See also Pierce, "Politics of Esther and Mordecai," 84.

46. Laffey, *Wives, Harlots and Concubines*, 216.

2

Esther & the Covenant

In the previous chapter several aspects of Esther 2 were seen to give us considerable doubt about the piety and devotion of Esther and Mordecai. The moral fiber of our protagonists was shown to be, at best, questionable and ambiguous. But what about those parts in the story that seem to suggest that they were committed to God after all, such as Mordecai's refusal to bow to Haman (3:4), Mordecai's confidence that deliverance will come for the Jews "from another place" (4:14), Esther's three-day fast (4:16), the possibility that the Jews engaged in a "holy war" against their enemies (8:15—9:19), or the fact that the book of Esther is ultimately about the inauguration of the religious holiday Purim (9:20–32)? These are the questions that the present chapter seeks to address. Do we, in fact, have evidence that Esther and Mordecai were committed to their covenant God, even if such commitment arose after turning back to God in repentance? I will contend that, in each case, the answer is an unequivocal no. Thus, in conjunction with the previous chapter we will see that the Jewish characters are consistently portrayed as secular and assimilated.

Mordecai's Refusal to Bow

After Mordecai uncovered and thwarted a plot to kill the king (2:21–23) the reader is surprised to find that a hitherto un-introduced character had been promoted within the ranks of the Persian Empire—Haman (3:1). As a result of the promotion, the king commanded that all of his officials were to bow before Haman (3:2). Yet Mordecai refused, claiming his Jewishness as the reason for his disobedience (3:2–4). But why exactly did Mordecai refuse to bow?

Mordecai did not bow, as he told the others, because he was a Jew (3:4). Many suppose therefore that Mordecai's refusal had religious connotations.[1] The common assumption is that Mordecai was, as a good Jew, avoiding idolatry. The Ten Commandments themselves prohibit bowing down to other gods and idols (Exod 20:5). So it is thought that Mordecai was expressing his devotion to God here. Note the interpretation offered by J. G. McConville:

> [Mordecai] *perceived* obeisance to Haman to be impossible in view of his higher loyalty. He was thus in the same position that Daniel was in when an embargo was laid upon prayer to God (Dan 6.6–9). Daniel must yet pray (Dan 6.10); and Mordecai must be faithful too to the God of his fathers, and the present generation of his people.[2]

Reidar Bjornard similarly asserts, "A good Jew can worship the covenant God only."[3] Likewise, Charles Swindoll writes, "To a Jew, bowing down to any person or thing on this earth was considered idolatry. It went against the deepest convictions of his faith."[4]

There are several problems, however, with assuming that Mordecai's motivation was religious. First, Mordecai was in a position of authority before the confrontation with Haman. He "sat in the king's gate" (2:19, 21), which was often where administrative offices were found.[5] Esther 3:2 implies, as well, that he was one of the "royal officials" required to bow down before Haman.[6] The Greek historian Herodotus wrote about Persian greetings, "A man of greatly inferior rank prostrates himself in profound reverence" (*Histories*, 1.134). In order for Mordecai to have attained his position

---

1. So Goldingay, *Ezra, Nehemiah, and Esther*, 167; Breneman, *Ezra, Nehemiah, Esther*, 327; Keil and Delitzsch, *Commentary on the Old Testament*, 343; Barnes, "Esther," 494; Semenye, "Esther," 562; McGee, *Ruth and Esther*, 259; *idem, Thru the Bible*, 558.

2. McConville, *Ezra, Nehemiah, and Esther*, 166 (emphasis original).

3. Bjornard, "Esther," 4.

4. Swindoll, *Esther*, 63. In fact, Swindoll (*Esther*, 70) finds a devotional insight here in Haman's response to Mordecai, telling his audience, "Never forget there will always be someone who will resent your devotion to the Lord."

5. Fox, *Character and Ideology*, 38.

6. Berlin (*Esther*, 31) suggests in the light of the fact that he overheard the plot to kill the king in Esther 2:21–23 that Mordecai was a member of the king's secret police.

within the Persian Empire, he would have had to show deference to the king on multiple occasions, which undoubtedly included prostration.

Second, and more importantly, the Old Testament itself never prohibits such activity. All throughout the Old Testament we find examples of various figures bowing down or prostrating to others without such activity being offered as worship by the one bowing or being perceived as such by the one revered. Take a look at these examples:

- Abraham bowed before the Hittites (Gen 23:7).

- Jacob bowed down to Esau seven times; Jacob's family (Leah, Rachel, and their children) bowed as well (Gen 33:3, 6–7).

- The brothers of Joseph bowed down before him (Gen 42:6; 43:28).

- A prophecy declared that the sons of Judah's father would bow down to Judah (Gen 49:8).

- Moses bowed down to Jethro, his father-in-law (Exod 18:7).

- David bowed down before Jonathan three times (1 Sam 20:41).

- David prostrated before Saul (1 Sam 24:8).

- Abigail bowed before David (1 Sam 25:23) and before David's servants (1 Sam 25:41).

- Saul bowed before the spirit of Samuel (1 Sam 28:14).

- An Amalekite bowed to David (2 Sam 1:2).

- Absalom bowed down before his father King David (2 Sam 14:33).

- Ziba bowed to David (2 Sam 16:4).

- A Cushite bowed before Joab (2 Sam 18:21).

- Shimei fell prostrate before King David (2 Sam 19:18).

- Bathsheba bowed down before King David (1 Kgs 1:16, 31).

- Nathan bowed before King David (1 Kgs 1:23).

- Adonijah bowed before Solomon (1 Kgs 1:53).

- Obadiah bowed to Elijah (1 Kgs 18:7).

- Prophets from Jericho bowed before Elisha (2 Kgs 2:15).

- Araunah the Jebusite bowed to David (1 Chr 21:21).

- Kings bow down before the king of Israel (Ps 72:9, 11).

- The kings of the nations will bow down before Israel (Isa 45:14).

- Princes will bow down before the servant of the Lord (Isa 49:7).

- Kings and queens will bow before Israel (Isa 49:23).

- The children of Israel's oppressors will bow down before Israel (Isa 60:14).

- The Lord commands the Kingdom of Judah to bow its neck to Nebuchadnezzar (Jer 27:8–11). Nebuchadnezzar prostrates before Daniel (Dan 2:46).

In a few instances we also find people bowing down before angelic beings, and if bowing down is a sign of worship, then even reverence to divine beings other than yhwh would be problematic. For example, Daniel bowed before the angelic figure Gabriel "who looked like a man" (Dan 8:15–17). We likewise see several people bow before the Angel of the Lord, including Balaam (Num 22:31) and Joshua (Josh 5:14), as well as David and the elders (1 Chr 21:16). When we look at the story of Esther itself we see Esther fall prostrate before the king (Esth 8:3). Thus, prostration and obeisance toward other humans was often a sign of respect for authority, though not exclusively so. In Esther 3 it was surely a sign of honor to go with the promotion of Haman.

So if we can conclude that Mordecai's refusal to bow was not *religiously* motivated, what other motivations could have been involved? It is possible that the answer is simply pride.[7] Perhaps Mordecai was upset that Haman was promoted instead of himself; he did save the king's life after all (see 2:21–23). Yet the reason Mordecai gives for not bowing in 3:4 is that he was a Jew. What this likely means, then, is that Mordecai's decision was rooted in *ethnic/ancestral* motivations.

Haman is referred to as an "Agagite" throughout Esther (3:1, 10; 8:3, 5; 9:24). The title recalls Agag, who was king of the Amalekites when Saul was king of Israel, and Saul was one of Mordecai's ancestors (see pp. 19–20). The progenitor of the Amalekites, Amalek, was a son of Esau (Gen 36:12) and so the tradition of sibling rivalry between Jacob and Esau is in the background. More specifically, hostility between Israel and the Amalekites is found throughout the Old Testament. After the exodus, while Israel was wandering in the desert, they were attacked by the Amalekites (Exod 17:8–15). This was the first hostile event that Israel had experienced after the exodus and it served to establish a severe animosity with the Amalekites.

---

7. Waltke and Yu, *Old Testament Theology*, 767; J. Martin, "Esther," 705; Huey, "Esther," 812; *idem*, "Irony as the Key," 37.

The Lord told Moses in response, "I will completely blot out the name of Amalek from under heaven" (Exod 17:14) and it was explained that "the LORD will be at war against the Amalekites from generation to generation" (Exod 17:16). In Deuteronomy the Lord reminds Israel of what the Amalekites did to them and tells them to remember to blot out Amalek (Deut 25:17–19). The Amalekites were also part of the indigenous dwellers in the promised land before Israel's conquest (Num 13:29; 14:25). Just before the conquest, some Israelites preemptively went to attack those within the land, including the Amalekites, although Moses advised them not to, and they were destroyed (Num 14:41–45). Throughout Israel's history they remained perennially at war with the Amalekites (Judg 3:13; 5:14; 6:3, 33; 7:12; 10:12; 1 Sam 30:1–2; 2 Sam 1:1; 1 Chr 4:43; Ps 83:7). However, Balaam had prophesied that Israel's king would one day be greater than Agag (Num 24:7), and that Amalek would be utterly destroyed (Num 24:20). This means that Mordecai had both a corporate ethnic prejudice against Haman (Israel vs. Amalek) and a more specific ancestral prejudice due to their respective genealogies (Saul vs. Agag). So when we come to Mordecai's refusal to bow to Haman we can see that their respective ancestry assumes a great history of animosity and we need not assume that religious convictions, especially an aversion to idolatry, played a role.[8] We will return once more to the conflict between Saul and Agag at the end of the chapter.

The central conflict of the story of Esther—Haman's plot to kill all the Jews—was therefore provoked singularly by Mordecai's refusal to bow (3:5–6). This single act of defiance clearly did not warrant the plot of such a great massacre, but when Mordecai's actions are read as another conflict in a long history of animosity, a bit more rationale is provided. So the background of the Israelite-Amalekite conflict not only offers the best explanation of Mordecai's refusal to bow, but also Haman's quick decision to retaliate to such a disproportionately higher degree.

Haman cast *pur* (or lots) to determine which day he would destroy the Jews and the lot fell on the thirteenth of Adar (3:7). Haman was then able to convince the king to sign an edict calling for the complete destruction of all the Jews in every province. And not just some of them—*all of them* (3:12–14). He explained to the king that the Jews—whom he obliquely called "a certain people" who "keep themselves separate" (or, better, who

---

8. Firth (*Message of Esther*, 63) goes too far when he states, "[Mordecai] apparently would not honor someone when that meant contradicting God's declared opposition to Amalek." This gives the background of Mordecai's heritage a theological spin that is lacking from the stated convictions and motivations of Mordecai.

were *unassimilated*)—had their own laws, and did not keep the king's laws (3:8). The accusation here carries an ironic tone. Have Esther and Mordecai, as representative Jews in the story, shown themselves to be separate and unassimilated? Did they actually follow "their own laws"? And even though they do actually follow the king's laws—such as agreeing to comply with the king's decree to replace Vashti (2:1–18)—they show no sign of following *their King's laws*. When Mordecai refused to bow to Haman, the officials had to ask Mordecai "day after day" why he defied the law to show deference to Haman until he finally admitted it was because he was a Jew (3:4). Apparently, being "a Jew" did not leave an impression on them; the irony of Haman's accusations in 3:8, therefore, seems fairly clear.

So the king signed Haman's edict and it was sent to every province in every language on the thirteenth day of the first month of the year (3:12). This date was highly significant for Jews since that very night (days began at sundown for the Jews) would be the start of the celebration of Passover. This means that all of Esther 4:1–17, which depicts the response of the Jews to the announcement of Haman's edict, would have taken place on the first day of the Passover celebration. Whether they recognized this at all remains to be seen.

Weeping & Fasting: Esther Chapter 4

In the midst of the perilous news that an edict had been decreed in which every Jew was to be destroyed, we read of Mordecai professing great confidence that "relief and deliverance" will arise for the Jews "from another place" (4:14) and we finally see Esther take action into her own hands in resolving to go before the king to request his intervention, even though it was forbidden to go un-summoned—"if I perish, I perish" (4:16). Dramatic tension reaches to great heights here as Esther calls for a three-day fast in her honor (4:16). If one is prepared to see religious devotion in the book at all, it is certainly in this chapter.

A Scene of Repentance?

There are some interpreters who acknowledge various levels of compromise in the story (like the sort outlined in chapter one, *Esther & the Compromise*), yet maintain that the story of Esther contains moral development and transformation starting in Esther 4. For instance, J. Vernon McGee begins his commentary by arguing that the Jews in Susa "forgot God; they were far from Him."[9] Yet later, when commenting on Esther 4, McGee is able to assert, "Mordecai is becoming a noble man now in my estimation. He is revealing that he is taking a stand for God. He is willing to die for God."[10] Thus, McGee concludes, "Both Mordecai and Esther come on the page of Scripture in a poor light, although they prove to be very noble individuals."[11] Likewise, in Walvoord and Zuck's *Bible Knowledge Commentary*, we see a similar affirmation about the transformation of Mordecai that culminates in Esther 4: "Though Mordecai is not pictured as a pious man who was righteous in his dealings before God, he at least had a sense of the covenantal relationship between God and Israel."[12] Leland Ryken affirms as well that Esther begins with a "weak character" yet begins to develop "heroic moral stature" in this chapter.[13] Beth Moore likewise interprets Esther 4 as marking a return to God. The behavior of the Jews showed that they "understood their peril to be associated with their wanderings from God. They had become so worldly and so thoroughly assimilated into Persian culture that they'd lost their protective shield."[14] This perspective on Esther 4 was similarly expressed by Mark Driscoll in his eleven-part sermon series from 2012: Esther begins the story as a "hypocrite,"[15] then chapter 4 functions as a "hinge"[16] so that by the end of the story Esther becomes one of the godliest women—"We all agree on that."[17] Driscoll therefore concludes

---

9. McGee, *Thru the Bible*, 544–45.

10. Ibid., 564.

11. McGee, *Ruth and Esther*, 244.

12. J. Martin, "Esther," 707.

13. Ryken, *Words of Delight*, 118, cited in Jobes, *Esther*, 146.

14. B. Moore, *Esther*, 85.

15. He explains, "She says she belongs to God, but she disobeys his dietary laws in Scripture. She says she belongs to God, but she lives far away from him. She says she belongs to God, but at this point, we've never seen her pray, open the Bible, worship God, repent of sin. No indication that she has any relationship with God whatsoever." See Driscoll, *Esther*, pt. 3, "Jesus Is a Better Savior."

16. Driscoll, *Esther*, pt. 5, "Jesus Is a Better Mediator."

17. Driscoll, *Esther*, pt. 3, "Jesus Is a Better Savior." This is unpacked elsewhere in the series by suggesting that Esther displays the fruit of the Spirit from Galatians 5:22–23 as she comes into her own faith (see Driscoll, *Esther*, pt. 6, "Jesus Gives a Better Identity"), and that Esther and Mordecai become missionaries at the end of the story (see Driscoll, *Esther*, pt. 9, "Jesus Is a Better Missionary").

from the story of Esther a paradigm of repentance—"Our part, friends, is repentance. God's part is reversal."[18]

However, interpreting Esther 4 in a religious manner, as a scene of repentance or otherwise, has serious deficiencies. What exactly did Mordecai mean by saying that help will come from another place? What is this *other place*? Why is Mordecai so confident here? Can we be sure that this is in fact an assertion of confidence? And what are we to make of the fasting and weeping in this chapter? These are the sorts of questions that we will try to tackle as we attempt to understand this pivotal chapter.

What Does "From Another Place" Mean? (Esther 4:14)

As we begin to take a deeper look at verse 14, we should stop and read verses 13–14 to see Mordecai's full response to Esther's initial hesitancy to go before the king un-summoned:

> Do not think that because you are in the king's house you alone of all the Jews will escape. For if you remain silent at this time, relief and deliverance for the Jews will arise from another place, but you and your father's family will perish. And who knows but that you have come to your royal position for such a time as this? (Esth 4:13–14)

For many, such as Carey Moore, "from another place" is thought to be a "veiled allusion to God."[19] This has been suggested because some later rabbinic texts refer to God as "the Place,"[20] and, more broadly speaking, the presence of God is often manifested in particular places, such as Zion and the Temple Mount.

It is possible that the use of "place" in Esther was intended as a circumlocution for God, a word presumably used to avoid causing offense. Of course, the third commandment from the Ten Commandments specifically forbade the misuse of God's name (Exod 20:7; Deut 5:11), and such resulted in execution by stoning in some instances (Lev 24:10–23). Among the manuscripts found at Qumran near the Dead Sea was a document known as *The Community Rule* (1QS), presumably utilized to govern the daily life of the sectarian community that occupied the nearby site. In this document

18. Driscoll, *Esther*, pt. 10, "Jesus Is a Better Reversal."
19. C. Moore, *Esther*, 50.
20. Berlin and Brettler, *Jewish Study Bible*, 1631. See also *Gen. Rab.* 68.

we find that even uttering the name of God on accident was grounds for expulsion from the group!

> If any man has uttered the [Most] Venerable Name even though frivolously, or as a result of shock or for any other reason whatever, while reading the Book or blessing, he shall be dismissed and shall return to the Council of the Community no more. (1QS VI 27b—VII 2a)[21]

Since uttering the name of God (YHWH) was considered problematic to many Jews it is possible that the word "place" was used as a way of referring to God using other words.

But if the author did want his readers to think of God here, and if this is what Mordecai's words mean, then why do we not find this to be more explicit and simple? Why are these words so ambiguous? As an answer to this, J. G. McConville asserts that the lack of direct reference to God "is deliberate, and the reason, paradoxically, is precisely to *affirm* God's activity behind events."[22] I would agree that there is something deliberate going on here in Esther, yet it is hardly convincing that this deliberation—to remove explicit reference to God—is somehow meant to *affirm* God's activity. Seems sort of counterproductive, does it not?

At this point another problem emerges because Mordecai mentions help from *another* place, which, if the reference to "place" was intended to be a reference to God, this implies that Mordecai anticipates another god to come to the rescue (or that somehow Esther is equal to God).[23] The use of the adjective *another* seems to make any suggestion of divinity implied by the term "place" implausible.

Nevertheless many still see an oblique reference to God in this verse. The way this is typically imagined is that Mordecai's words could reflect his belief that God will indeed act, by whatever means possible, utilizing whomever he pleases, to ensure the redemption of his people.[24] Representative of this perspective is Mervin Breneman, who asserts, "Mordecai's

---

21. Vermes, *Complete Dead Sea Scrolls*, 107.

22. McConville, *Ezra, Nehemiah, and Esther*, 173 (emphasis original).

23. Fox (*Character and Ideology*, 63) notes, "If God is *another* place, then Esther is herself 'a place,' meaning that they are on the same plane—two distinct loci of salvation—and that is not conceivable" (emphasis original).

24. Webb, *Five Festal Garments*, 123; Goldingay, *Ezra, Nehemiah, and Esther*, 172; Schultz, "Book of Esther," 62; Levenson, *Esther*, 19; Baldwin, *Esther*, 79–80; Swindoll, *Esther*, 85.

statement reveals a deep conviction of God's providence, a belief that God rules in the world, even in the details of the nations and in the lives of individuals."[25] Thus, "another place" may refer to another human figure that God appoints to bring about "relief and deliverance."[26]

Despite each of the attempts to find God veiled behind Mordecai's "another place," none of them are ultimately convincing. What makes this interpretation even less likely is the possibility that the traditional translation of 4:14 is wrong. Rather than reading Mordecai's words as a statement—*relief and deliverance will arise from another place*—I want to explain why I think these words are better rendered as a rhetorical question expecting a negative answer. When these words are recognized as a question it is clear that Mordecai's words are not a veiled reference to God, and neither do they convey confidence or assurance. It is to this discussion that we now turn.

Will Help Come "From Another Place"? (Esther 4:14)

One of the things that the traditional reading of 4:14 cannot explain adequately is how Mordecai is certain that if Esther does not go to the king that she would perish along with her household, but the rest of the Jews would be delivered. Some who follow a traditional interpretation of 4:14 try to avoid the discrepancy by understanding Mordecai's words as a belief in divine retribution.[27] But there is no reason to insert God at this point, and the book of Esther taken as a whole should point us in the opposite direction. Others see a reference to future retribution by the Jews who will experience deliverance,[28] possibly because they would then view Esther as an enemy since she did not identify with them in their plight. It has also been suggested that Mordecai himself was threatening to kill Esther.[29] This last suggestion would be the most plausible—since it does not infer the actions of others for which there is no evidence—if it were not for the fact that Mordecai is part of Esther's "father's family" and is therefore among those who will perish if Esther keeps quiet.

---

25. Breneman, *Ezra, Nehemiah, Esther*, 337.

26. Jobes, *Esther*, 133.

27. Clines, *Esther Scroll*, 36.

28. Webb, *Five Festal Garments*, 122.

29. Pierce, "Politics of Esther and Mordecai," 87.

Despite the attempts to nuance the traditional reading of 4:14, there is simply no satisfactory explanation for Mordecai's confidence that "relief and deliverance will arise for the Jews" and yet Esther and her "father's family" will perish.[30] The logical connection between the clauses is so unclear in verse 14 that the way we conceive of the passage begs for reconsideration.

Note how awkward the consensus reading is as it is rewritten in poetic form:

> He said, "If on this dark'ning day
> You hold your tongue, God will provide
> Protection from some other side,
> And you will die. [. . .]"[31]

Does the poetic structure and flow help you sense how much of a non sequitur Mordecai's words appear? Why will "God provide protection" but Esther "will die"? After hearing Mordecai's odd conclusion in Esther 4:14 we can almost imagine Esther thinking to herself afterwards:

> The Jewish people are going to live, no matter what I do; if I remain silent, they survive, and if I somehow do the impossible and convince the king, they survive. And, no matter what I do, I will die; if I remain silent, Mordecai says I will die, and if I go to the king un-summoned the law says I must die, and Persian laws cannot be repealed. So whether I remain silent or not, I will die, and the Jews will survive.

This internal commentary is meant to show the logical disjointedness of the traditional reading. Yet if we regard the key clause in 4:14 as a question some of the interpretive difficulties are assuaged.

In the written form of Biblical Hebrew, questions are often designated by a particular letter (*He*) at the start of an interrogative clause. This has a similar function in English to the placement of a question mark at the end of a sentence to indicate a question. Questions can also be introduced in English with certain words, such as, *who*, *when*, *where*, *why*, or *how*, and this is similar in Hebrew. In spoken English, as in Hebrew, questions are often detected by vocal intonation.

The clause in question—"relief and deliverance for the Jews will arise from another place"—does not have any key words normally utilized to

---

30. In the film *Book of Esther*, this tension is erased and the Jews will only perish if Esther is silent: "There is a time to remain silent and a time to speak, but if you remain silent now, you and your people will perish."

31. Piper, *Esther*, 54.

start a question. And so, virtually every major translation of Esther renders this clause as a statement (see NIV; HCSB; KJV; MESSAGE; NASB; NRSV; RSV; NKJV; NLT; NET). However, in Late Biblical Hebrew—in which, as a story dated to the fifth or fourth century BCE, Esther is written[32]—it became more and more customary to omit typical signs designated for questions (such as the interrogative *He*).[33] This is sort of analogous to how, in our modern era, emails and text messages written in English often do not contain question marks if it is obvious to the writer and/or the reader. It is precisely this issue of what is "obvious" that aids our discussion here. What makes a question "obvious" is context. In Esther 4:14 our options are either to stick with the traditional reading, which I have suggested is basically incoherent, or render the clause under discussion as a question.

Rendering 4:14b as a rhetorical question was first suggested in an article by John M. Wiebe and was later taken up in F. Bush's commentary on Esther.[34] In agreement with them, I think that the text should be rendered as a rhetorical question expecting a negative answer, "if you remain silent at this time, will relief and deliverance come from another source?" To make this more clear, since the rhetorical question anticipates a negative response, Bush's rendering inserts the negation into the text and removes the question: "For, if you remain silent at this time, relief and deliverance will not arise for the Jews from any other quarter, and you and your father's house will perish."[35] Essentially then, Mordecai is suggesting that Esther is the only hope for the Jews; he is not expressing faith in God's sovereignty here. If Esther keeps silent, all the Jews will die. Period. So although 4:14b does not contain the sorts of clues that we might expect for a question, the context warrants it; the interpretive difficulties are removed. Therefore, if we take Mordecai's words to be a rhetorical question implying a negative answer, then the death of Esther and her father's family (i.e., Mordecai) is

32. See Fox, *Character and Ideology*, 139–40. Yet Fox prefers a third-century date for Esther.

33. Wiebe, "Esther 4:14," 414–15; Bush, *Ruth, Esther*, 397. See also Gesenius, *Hebrew Grammar*, 473 (§150.1). Joüon and Muraoka (*Grammar of Biblical Hebrew*, 573–74 [§161a]) notes that for rhetorical questions a rise in intonation would be sufficient.

34. Wiebe, "Esther 4:14," 413; Bush, *Ruth, Esther*, 391. Breneman's dismissal of Wiebe's thesis is completely uncritical (*Ezra, Nehemiah, Esther*, 336); he deems it incorrect simply because it removes God from the equation. However, one must prove that God was a part of the equation in the first place! Regardless, none of his critiques engage the grammatical argument directly. See also Firth's quick dismissal (*Message of Esther*, 76 n. 24).

35. Bush, *Ruth, Esther*, 390.

dependent solely on Esther's inactivity, which keeps the imminent problem in view. Even if, however, the arguments that I have offered for interpreting 4:14b as an interrogative clause are found unconvincing, it would still be unwarranted to insert God into 4:14—either by divine deliverance for the Jews or divine retribution toward Esther if she keeps silent. So then, Mordecai does not assert confidence in God's providence here, but rather displays the opposite. Esther is the only hope, and there is nothing to suggest that Mordecai has any belief that God may indeed act to overcome the Jewish plight. His sentiment is the same as that expressed by Princess Leia—"Help me, Obi-Wan Kenobi. You're my only hope."[36]

Even though we have ruled out confidence in God from Mordecai's words, it would be incorrect to assert instead that the scene takes place at "the juncture between faith and agnosticism."[37] Mordecai was not struggling with God's absence; he appears to be indifferent to God's activity. Yet Esther's immediate response to Mordecai is to call a three-day fast (4:16). Indeed, when the Jews initially hear of the destruction that awaits them they wail and weep and fast (4:3). Are we not meant to read these verses as suggesting that Esther and the rest of the people of Israel were calling upon God for "relief and deliverance"?

What Is the Significance of "Fasting"? (Esther 4:16)

In *Esther and the King* (2010), a Mormon (LDS) film, fasting is the central focus. The opening segments depict a modern-day family (well, really a *Latter-day* family!) in which a little girl struggles to invite George, the family's butler, to church. While the daughter, Amelia, is getting ready for bed with her mother, she confesses that she keeps "chickening out" in her attempts to invite George, although she has also been praying about it. Amelia's mother then validates her, expressing how happy she is to know that her daughter has been praying. Her mother shares with her that there is something else that can help. "Sometimes," Amelia's mother explains, "when there's something that I really need the Lord's help with, something that needs a ton of faith, I fast." The mother then continues by telling Amelia that she would like to tell her a story to demonstrate this point, and this transitions into a reenactment of the Esther story. Once the Esther story concludes, a *fasting* Amelia and her family are shown leaving for church

36. *Star Wars Episode IV: A New Hope.*

37. Day, *Esther*, 92.

as George the butler joins in at the last minute, explaining how much he admired the little girl for fasting on his behalf, turning down his "world famous" silver dollar pancakes.

The film clearly suggests that fasting was practiced in order to make the prayers of the Jews more effective. Indeed many note that fasting is meaningless outside of religious intentions. For instance, Jon Levenson writes that a fast is "a totally impotent and senseless gesture if there is no higher power that it can influence."[38] Similarly, Charles Swindoll asserts, "The Jews didn't stop eating to lose weight; they fasted for spiritual reasons."[39] However, prayer is not mentioned anywhere in Esther 4 (or anywhere else in the book for that matter). So some suggest that prayer is at least implied.[40] Yet others make much more explicit claims, such as, "The power of prayer is plainly taught."[41] Levenson notes that the reversal of the plight of the Jews in the story makes it likely that "the author wants us to suspect that this was indeed partially in response to the extraordinary penitential exercises of Mordecai, Esther, and the rest of the Jewish people."[42] In the same vein, Joyce Baldwin asserts, "The whole point of fasting was to render the prayer experience more effective and prepare oneself for communion with God."[43] For Gary Smith, fasting was a way for Esther "to prepare her heart (4:16) and seek the merciful intervention of God."[44] Even L. B. Paton, for whom the book of Esther is essentially nonreligious, regards fasting to be "the only religious rite" in the story,[45] and later states that it was designed to "propitiate God."[46]

Yet fasting in and of itself is not inherently religious. As Adele Berlin notes, "Fasting and sackcloth are probably not to be seen as specifically Jewish religious practices, but as universal expressions of mourning in the ancient Near East."[47] Despite the claims of Joyce Baldwin that prayer "is al-

38. Levenson, *Esther*, 19.

39. Swindoll, *Esther*, 97.

40. Bjornard, "Esther," 13; Larson and Dahlen, *Ezra, Nehemiah, Esther*, 320; Baldwin, *Esther*, 31; B. Moore, *Esther*, 100; Bush, *Ruth, Esther*, 398.

41. Demaray, "Esther," 675.

42. Levenson, *Esther*, 78.

43. Baldwin, *Esther*, 80.

44. Smith, *Ezra, Nehemiah, Esther*, 258.

45. Paton, *Critical and Exegetical Commentary*, 96.

46. Ibid., 225.

47. Berlin, *Esther*, 45.

ways the accompaniment of fasting in the Old Testament,"[48] there are a few clear examples in the Old Testament where fasting is not accompanied by prayer or other distinctly religious activity. For instance, one wonders how genuine Jezebel's call to fast actually was (see 1 Kgs 21:9, 12). The clearest examples, though, of nonreligious fasting are when fasting is depicted in relation to someone who has died. In 1 Samuel 31:13 and 1 Chronicles 10:12 we read about the camp of Israel fasting for seven days after the death of Saul and his sons, and similarly in 2 Samuel 1:12 David and those with him fasted until night upon hearing this news. Later, David tells Joab to tear his clothes, put on sackcloth, and walk in mourning in front of Abner's dead body (2 Sam 3:31). David then "fasts" until sunset (2 Sam 3:35) and takes an oath that God should harm him if he eats something; but it is interesting that he was not fasting to gain any sort of activity from God. It is part of a lament for a dead friend.[49] In an Egyptian text known as *The Prophecies of Neferti*—most likely dated from 1999 to 1960 BCE—we read about lament not being carried out properly in the face of disaster:

> One will laugh at distress;
> None will weep over death,
> None spends the night fasting because of death,
> The heart of a man cares only for himself.
> Mourning is no (longer) carried out today,
> Hearts have quite abandoned it.[50]

What is worth pointing out here is the fact that fasting could be a typical response to lamentable situations in the ancient Near East and was not exclusively a means of petitioning a deity.

To be sure, there are more examples of fasting occurring in religious contexts in the Old Testament than otherwise (see Judg 20:26; 1 Sam 7:6; 2 Sam 12:16, 21–23; 1 Kgs 21:27; 2 Kgs 18:6; 2 Chr 20:3; Ezra 8:21, 23; 9:5; Neh 1:4; 9:1; Ps 35:13; 69:10; 109:24; Isa 58:3–6; Jer 14:12; 36:6, 9; Dan 9:3; Joel 1:14; 2:12, 15; Jonah 3:5; Zech 7:5; 8:19). But this is precisely the point: is Esther 4 a religious context? Just as the prophet Zechariah asked the people of Israel on behalf of God—"When you fasted and mourned . . . was it really for me that you fasted?" (Zech 7:5)—we are justified in wondering

---

48. Baldwin, *Esther*, 80.

49. There was customary food for mourners as well. See Jer 16:7; Ezek 24:17, 22; Hos 9:4.

50. Hallo and Younger, *Context of Scripture*, 1.45 (within lines 40–45), translated by Nili Shupak.

the same question regarding Esther 4.[51] Fasting is not sufficient to make Esther 4 a religious context, we need the religious context first in order to interpret the fasting as religious.

The biggest problem with interpreting Esther's fast as religious is the fact that she calls her handmaidens to fast with her—"I and my attendants will fast as you do" (Esth 4:16). Most commentators move far too quickly past this point when addressing the fasting of Esther's handmaidens. It is incredibly unlikely that any of these women were Jewish, let alone all of them. For this reason, those who have taken this reference seriously have proposed some rather speculative reconstructions. For instance, Mervin Breneman writes, "This meant [Esther] would share her faith with these maids."[52] The insertion of faith here is unwarranted and is based purely on the assumption that fasting is necessarily religious (not to mention specifically Jewish). Rather we are meant to see in this inclusion of the maids that the nature of the fasting was not designed to petition the God of Israel. Calling upon the maidens to fast either makes such an action syncretistic, or shows that it was secular.

I suggest, therefore, that Esther's call to fast was intended as a corporate lament for Esther's imminent death—"if I perish, I perish" (4:16). There is likely something analogous between this scene and the way Jephthah's daughter mourned her imminent death for two months in a similar ascetic ("roaming the hills") and corporate ("with my friends") manner (see Judg 11:37–39). Mourning in the ancient Near East was ultimately part of a "ritual identification with the dead."[53] This is seen, not least in sackcloth as the clothing of the dead—as well in the use of ashes and dust which is the state that the dead have been consigned to—but also in fasting itself which is a "similar life-denying mourning ritual."[54] Just as 1 Samuel 31:13, 2 Samuel 1:12, and 1 Chronicles 10:12 depict people fasting in response to the death of Saul and his sons, it is conceivable that Esther's fast was a lament for the inescapable. Thus, I do not regard the fast as preventive, but

---

51. If God can critique the motivations of Israel's fasting (see Isa 58:3–7) this implies that there are right and wrong ways to fast; motivations can be called into question (see Jer 14:12).

52. Breneman, *Ezra, Nehemiah, Esther*, 337.

53. Laniak, *Shame and Honor*, 93.

54. See Laniak, *Shame and Honor*, 93, following G. Anderson (*Time to Mourn*) and others. However, Laniak regards the fast in 4:16 as religious and preventive (wrongly, in my view).

rather as a concession. Esther called on others to fast with her out of ritual solidarity for what was likely an inevitable death—and the dead do not eat.

There is, however, one final issue to address in regards to the fourth chapter of Esther; this is the suggestion that this chapter develops the theology of the prophet Joel as a way to show that the fasting in question was indeed designed to implore divine activity, even though neither prayer nor God himself are mentioned.

A Reference to Joel 2?

Karen Jobes has made the case that Esther 4 is written in such a way that shows dependence on Joel 2. The importance of this link for interpreting Esther 4, as Jobes explains, is that it shows how Esther's intent in calling a fast was to call upon God to act on behalf of her people.

The correspondences between Joel 2 and Esther 4 are worth listing here:

1. *The specific terms used*: Joel 2:12 calls for the people to "return to me with all your heart, with fasting and weeping and mourning" and Esther 4:3 speaks of the Jews in all the provinces "fasting, weeping, and wailing"; thus, the two texts have the same three Hebrew words in consecutive order (ṣôm, bᵉkî, mispēḏ).[55]

2. *The idiom "who knows"*: Joel 2:14 reads, "Who knows? He may turn and relent" and in Esther 4:14 Mordecai asks Esther, "And who knows but that you have come to your royal position for such a time as this?"[56]

3. *The calling of a fast*: Joel 2:15 reads, "Blow the trumpet in Zion; sanctify a fast" and in Esther 4:16 we have the dramatic account of Esther calling a three day fast for all the Jewish people to partake in.[57]

Look at the following figure for the correspondences between Joel 2 and Esther 4:

---

55. Jobes, *Esther*, 135.
56. Ibid., 137.
57. Ibid.

Joel 2:12–15	Esther 4:3, 14, 16
(12) Yet even now, says the LORD,	(3) In every province to which the edict and order of the king came, there was
return to me with all your heart, *with fasting, with weeping, and with mourning*; (13) rend your hearts and not your clothing. Return to the LORD, your God . . .	great mourning among the Jews, *with fasting and weeping and wailing*. Many lay in sackcloth and ashes.
(14) *Who knows?* He may turn and relent and leave a blessing—grain offerings and drink offerings for the LORD your God.	(14) And *who knows* but that you have come to your royal position for such a time as this?
(15) Blow the trumpet in Zion, *declare a holy fast*; call a *sacred assembly*.	(16) "Go, *gather together all the Jews* who are in Susa, and *fast* for me. Do not eat or drink for three days, night or day. I and my attendants fast as you do"

In addition to these points made by Jobes, I would like to add a pair of corresponding themes that make the case for the reuse of Joel 2 even more convincing.

4. *The preservation of life*: Joel 2:17 records the ministers in the temple praying, "Spare your people," and naturally, the whole conflict of Esther chapter 4 is about the imminent genocide of the Jewish people.

5. *Conflict with the nations*: The destruction of the Jews by Haman in Esther is paralleled thematically by Joel's fear that the Jewish people will become a mockery among the nations if God does not act. The nations will ask, "Where is their God?" (Joel 2:17). As we have seen, this question regarding the absence of God is particularly apt for the story of Esther.

In the light of these correspondences, one may be tempted to conclude with Jobes that "whether Esther was mindful of Joel's prophecy or not, she in effect 'blows the trumpet in Zion,' commanding Mordecai to call a fast for all the Jews of Susa, to see if the Lord may relent from sending this calamity on her people."[58] Yet the problem with this interpretation is that

---

58. Jobes, *Esther*, 137. Beth Moore also agrees with the connection to Joel 2:12 in Esth 4:3 (*Esther*, 84).

it assumes that one of the critical missing pieces in the correspondences between Joel 2 and Esther 4—namely, repentance—is in fact part of the progression depicted in Esther. This is simply not the case. Instead of *rent hearts*, as Joel 2:13 calls for, we simply read about rent clothing and sack-cloth (Esther 4:1, 3).[59] We are not told that the Jews cried out to the Lord for help or that they held any optimistic views about God's ability to act on their behalf if they repented. I have already tried to demonstrate that Mor-decai's famous words in 4:14 do not convey confidence in God, and there is no reason to insert prayer or repentance into the activity surrounding the fasts of chapter 4.

However, it has been noted by some that the idiom "who knows" from 4:14 has positive and optimistic connotations elsewhere. Thus, Jon Leven-son concludes, "In several other passages in the Hebrew Bible, these words preface a guarded hope that penitential practice may induce God to relent from his harsh decree, granting deliverance where destruction had been expected."[60] Yet, as we will see, when we look at other passages where the idiom "who knows" occurs within a context of fasting—2 Samuel 12 and Jonah 3—*it is coupled with repentance in each case* just as in Joel 2. This makes the context of Esther 4 stand out.

We will begin with the text of 2 Samuel 12. This is the famous scene where Nathan the prophet confronts King David after the infamous affair with Bathsheba. Sadly, as a consequence of their sin, the child they con-ceived did not live past his first week. Note how the scene unfolds in regards to the function of fasting, lamenting, and sackcloth:

> David pleaded with God for the child. He fasted and spent the nights lying in sackcloth on the ground. [After hearing of the child's death] David got up from the ground. After he had washed, put on lotions and changed his clothes, he went into the house of the LORD and worshipped. Then he went to his own house, and at his request they served him food and he ate. His attendants asked him, "Why are you acting this way? While the child was alive you fasted and wept, but now that the child is dead, you get up and eat!" He answered, "While the child was still alive, I fasted and wept. I thought, 'Who knows? The LORD may be gracious to me and let the child live.' But now that he is dead, why should I go on fasting?" (2 Sam 12:16, 20–23a)

59. This was pointed out to me by Ernest Clark Jr.

60. Levenson, *Esther*, 81.

What we can see here is how repentance, worship, and seeking grace were intimately connected to David's remorseful petitioning for his son's life. Does this scene look similar to Esther 4 to you?

Turning to the text of Jonah 3:5–9 we see something very similar to 2 Samuel 12. Here Jonah has just spoken a message of judgment to the Ninevites, and we read:

> The Ninevites believed God. A fast was proclaimed, and all of them, from the greatest to the least, put on sackcloth. When Jonah's warning reached the king of Nineveh, he rose from his throne, took off his royal robes, covered himself with sackcloth and sat down in the dust. This is the proclamation he issued in Nineveh: "By the decree of the king and his nobles: Do not let people or animals, herds or flocks, taste anything; do not let them eat or drink. But let people and animals be covered with sackcloth. Let everyone call urgently on God. Let them give up their evil ways and their violence. Who knows? God may yet relent and with compassion turn from his fierce anger so that we will not perish." (Jonah 3:5–9)

Again, we can see how repentance was connected to the expectation that God might relent. This is something entirely missing from the Esther narrative, though it is present in Joel 2, 2 Samuel 12, and Jonah 3. Indeed, the connections regarding the rhetorical question "who knows," fasting, the appropriation of clothing for mourning, and other lament imagery are staggering in all four instances. Yet what is present in Jonah 3, 2 Samuel 12, and Joel 2 that is surprisingly missing from Esther 4 is the most important thing of all: repentance.

Passover?

To go a step further, there is another crucial element of Jewish life missing from this chapter. In addition to the deliberate omission of God, prayer, and repentance, we also see that there is not a hint that any of the Jews recognized what day it is. As already noted, Haman's edict was declared "on the thirteenth day of the first month" (3:12), which means that the Festival of Passover would begin that night (the night of Esther 4).[61] The Passover

---

61. Bush, *Ruth, Esther*, 398; Fox, *Character and Ideology*, 54. Samuel Wells, who regards Purim as a "parody" of the Passover tradition (see Wells and Sumner, *Esther & Daniel*, 10), states elsewhere, "It is as if a gauntlet has been laid at the feet of the God of Israel and the Passover tradition in which the action of God has been definitely discerned.

lamb was to be slaughtered at twilight on the fourteenth day of the first month (Exod 12:6; Lev 23:5; Num 9:3; 28:16; 33:3; 2 Chr 35:1; Ezra 6:19; Ezek 45:21),[62] and the festival was to last for seven days (Exod 12:15, 18; 13:6; 23:15; 34:18; Lev 23:6; Num 28:17; Deut 16:8; Ezra 6:22; Ezek 45:21). The Passover was intended to be celebrated as "a lasting ordinance" in commemoration of the exodus—God's deliverance of Israel from out of Egypt (Exod 12:14; see also 13:9–10). The celebration of Passover was therefore a *command* with specific stipulations (Exod 23:15; 34:18; Lev 23:4–8; Num 9:3; 28:16–25; Deut 16:1–8). These stipulations were not simply requirements if one had decided to observe Passover; the celebration of Passover in its proper manner was a command of God.[63]

At a time when the great deeds of the exodus would have been retold, when the sovereignty of God over foreign threats would have been proclaimed, and when the deliverance of Israel would have been relished in, the Jews in Susa showed no trust in God and no sense of confidence. The words of Judges seem to be an appropriate description of Esther and her generation as well—"After that whole generation had been gathered to their ancestors, another generation grew up who knew neither the LORD nor what he had done for Israel" (Judg 2:10). Why do we not read in Esther 4 of the Jews crying out, "*Remember your covenant, O Lord, as you did when we were in Egypt!*" (see Exod 2:24; 6:5)? Despite the glaring omission, Beth Moore imagines the Jews asking themselves, "*Why must we receive this terrifying news today of all days—on our own Passover?*"[64] But the absence of this question is quite telling. The absence, as well, of prayer and repentance

---

What use Passover, the narrative seems to say, when the Jews are all set to be wiped out before they next celebrate it? The Jews need rapidly to invent a new form of redemption, because if they wait for God's redemption, as disclosed through the Passover, to take effect, it will in all likelihood be too late." See Wells and Sumner, *Esther & Daniel*, 47. However, the omission of Passover celebration seems not to indict *the Passover* but rather those who ought to be celebrating it and finding in it an analogue for their current experience.

62. *Passover Letter* (3.46 in Hallo and Younger, *Context of Scripture*), dated to the late fifth century BCE, states that Passover was to be celebrated on the fourteenth of Nisan at twilight.

63. There is one interesting example of the Passover not being celebrated at the proper time. During Hezekiah's reign the Passover had to be celebrated during the second month of the year because there were not enough consecrated priests (2 Chr 30:1–5). However, Hezekiah still made sure that the Passover was celebrated; the Passover lamb was slaughtered on the fourteenth day of the second month (2 Chr 30:15) and the celebration lasted seven days as prescribed (2 Chr 30:21).

64. B. Moore, *Esther*, 74 (emphasis original).

is all the more staggering when it becomes evident that Esther's three-day fast would have occurred during the Passover festival, and yet no one recalled the mighty acts of God for comfort at that dark hour.

So up to this point in the narrative of Esther we have no reason to assume that Esther or Mordecai have much faith at all. They seem to have forgotten their covenant God—the God who promised Abraham that he would preserve them (Gen 12:1–3) and the God who entered a covenant relationship with Israel after preserving them in the exodus (see Exod 19–20). Perhaps something will change in the second half of the story? If, as some suggested, the fourth chapter of Esther marks a religious turning point in the narrative we should expect to see evidence of such a transition. Perhaps this is ultimately how they secured their military victory—by relying on their covenant God?

Holy War?

It may be easy to forget that the story of Esther does not end with the defeat of Haman. Once he is impaled on a pole intended for Mordecai at the end of chapter 7, there are still three chapters left! Because the text tells us that Persian laws cannot be repealed (8:8), the thirteenth of Adar still looms ominously over the story. Perhaps many are surprised when they read how the story *actually* ends: with two days of battle instead of one and a 75,810 body count, including Haman's ten sons, who—although already dead— were impaled as public spectacles (9:13).

In fact, many of the popular versions of Esther act as if chapter 9 was never written. In the Mormon (LDS) film, *Esther and the King* (2010), the story ends with the king simply revoking his decree and extending his apologies to all the Jews in the land. And, in a very explicit manner, the end of the credits read, "To learn more about this story, we invite you to visit Esther 2–8 in the Bible." The cartoon versions similarly omit any final battle whatsoever, such as, the *Veggie Tales* version (2000) and *Animated Stories from the Bible: Esther* (1993). This is also true in the novels of Joan Wolf and Norah Lofts, where the tension simply ends with the king canceling the earlier decree.[65] There are other popular retellings of the Esther story that contain battles yet minimize the violence in some way, such as *One Night with the King* (2006), which simply makes a quick reference to Jewish defense on the thirteenth of Adar, but there is no mention of the second

---

65. Wolf, *Reluctant Queen*, 349; Lofts, *Esther*, 144.

day of fighting (see 9:13). This omission of the second day is paralleled in the TV mini-series, *The Bible: Esther* (1999), and the report of the death toll is also considerably diminished—"hundreds of people have been killed on both sides."

Those who try to make sense of the battles in terms of the traditional reading of Esther usually regard the war in Esther 9 as a "holy war."[66] However, the notion of "holy war" inappropriately evokes the divine. How can such a war, in a book with assimilated characters that have a complete lack of trust in their covenant God, be called *holy*? If the battles were intended to function as a "holy war," where is the prayer for God's aid before the days of battle?[67] Or where is the doxology of praise following the victory? Why does Esther fail to offer a doxology like Deborah in Judges 5 after defeating her enemies? Or like David in 2 Samuel 22–23? Or like the one supplied in Gini Andrews's novel, *Esther: The Star and the Sceptre*, "Music and psalms and shouts of 'Victory for Adonai' came from Jewish homes"?[68] Can it genuinely be said, as in the comments of J. G. McConville, that the Jews were victors in the story of Esther "because of their reliance on God alone and because of their willingness"?[69] We see no examples of this.

Refusing to Take Plunder

Some point to the fact that the Jews refused to take plunder as an indication that they were partaking in a "holy war" (see 9:10, 15–16). Note the words of Jobes, "One of the rules of ancient holy war was that plunder must not be taken."[70] However, this misconstrues a few things. To start, it misconstrues the role of taking plunder more generally. Note these examples:

- When the Israelites destroyed the Midianites (Num 31) they were enacting "the LORD's vengeance" (Num 31:2–3) yet they took the plunder (Num 31:9, 11–12, 18) and divided it among themselves (Num 31:25–54).

- Israel also took plunder after the defeat of King Sihon of Heshbon (Deut 2:35), and King Og of Bashan (Deut 3:7).

---

66. E.g., Duguid, *Esther and Ruth*, 106–7; Jobes, *Esther*, 196.

67. Like the ones found in Andrews, *Esther*, 250, 257, and in *Bible: Esther* (1999).

68. Andrews, *Esther*, 264.

69. McConville, *Ezra, Nehemiah, and Esther*, 188–89.

70. Jobes, *Esther*, 196. See also Duguid, *Esther and Ruth*, 107.

- After Gideon killed Zebah and Zalmunnah he took the ornaments from their camels's necks (Judg 8:21), and he plundered the Ishmaelites (Judg 8:25–27).

- David and his men raided the Amalekites (1 Sam 27:8), and after attacking them at a later point (1 Sam 30:17) they re-plundered from the Amalekites what was stolen from David's camp (1 Sam 30:18–20).

- David received tribute from Moab (2 Sam 8:2) and Joram (2 Sam 8:9) and dedicated all the plunder he received to the Lord, including from Amalek (2 Sam 8:11–12).

- David took plunder from Ammonite towns (2 Sam 12:29–31).

- There are several other passages where taking plunder is clearly permitted (Deut 20:14–15; Josh 11:14; 22:8; 1 Sam 14:30, 32; 17:53; 2 Kgs 7:16; 1 Chr 20:2–3; 2 Chr 14:13; 20:25; 25:13; Ps 68:12; Isa 49:24–25; Ezek 39:10; Zeph 2:9).

Whenever taking plunder was ever prohibited, it was because the people were regarded as so vile that their possessions were likewise corrupt. In these instances, it was not simply that Israel was prohibited from taking the plunder, rather they were commanded to enact complete destruction, known as the ḥērem, or "the ban" (Deut 7:26; 13:12–18; 20:16–18; Josh 6:17–19, 21, 24; see also 1 Sam 15). This is why Achan's deeds after the Battle of Jericho were considered an act of unfaithfulness; and this was ultimately why Israel was not able to defeat Ai initially. Achan was not unfaithful merely for taking plunder, but because he had taken from the items that were to be devoted to complete destruction (Josh 7:1, 11–13, 15, 20–21; 22:20). Because of this, Achan was destroyed along with his entire household and possessions (Josh 7:24–26). After Achan was destroyed, the Israelites were able to defeat Ai and, interestingly, were permitted to take the plunder from Ai, although this was not permitted in regards to Jericho (Josh 8:2, 27). In total, there are not many examples where taking plunder is prohibited in the Old Testament.

This theme of not taking plunder, though, provides another interesting connection to the conflict between Haman and Mordecai. As already mentioned, Haman was an "Agagite" (3:1, 10; 8:3, 5; 9:24), meaning that he was a descendant of King Agag of Amalek. The most important biblical scene for King Agag is simultaneously the important scene for Mordecai's ancestor King Saul—1 Samuel 15.

After Saul defeated the Amalekites (1 Sam 14:48), the Lord spoke through Samuel, telling him that he must completely destroy the Amalekites because of what they did to Israel just after the exodus (1 Sam 15:2–3; see also Exod 17:8–16). Although Saul destroyed the city of Amalek, he kept King Agag alive along with some livestock (1 Sam 15:8–9, 15, 20–21). At once the Lord expressed his regret in appointing Saul king because of his disobedience (1 Sam 15:11). Samuel rebuked Saul for this (1 Sam 15:19, 22–23; 28:18) and it ultimately led to his rule over Israel being revoked. Then Samuel put King Agag to death (1 Sam 15:33). Ironically, Saul's life ended when he asked an anonymous Amalekite to kill him on the battlefield (2 Sam 1:9–10).

In the light of this background many note how the refusal to take plunder in the story of Esther expresses a reversal of the failures of King Saul against the Amalekites. It was—so the argument goes—descendants of King Saul who appear to finally get it right, taking out the Amalekites yet leaving the plunder alone. Sandra Berg concludes along these lines that forsaking the plunder reverses the situation of 1 Samuel 15.[71] Adele Berlin makes a similar comment: "It is as if the Jews in Mordecai's day are finally correcting the deficit that cost Saul his kingship."[72] Additionally, note the words of Lisa Wolfe: "It makes a striking connection to the misdeed of King Saul in 1 Samuel 15:1–35, where he did not 'utterly destroy' (*herem*) his Amelekite [*sic*] enemy. In that way, the Jews here are able to undo that ancestral error by decimating the Amelekites [*sic*] in this story."[73]

Yet there are three problems with this reading. The first problem is that the enemies of the Jews in Esther 9 were not Amalekites. These were simply enemies throughout all the provinces of the known world. Nothing is said about their nationalities, and the assumption that not laying a hand on the plunder reverses 1 Samuel 15 assumes that the war was against Amalekites when it was not.

Second, Saul was commanded to *destroy* everything in 1 Samuel 15, not simply leave the plunder alone. In the context of Esther it is clear that the concept of the *ḥērem*, or "the ban," is not present because we do not find complete destruction of the plunder.[74] In fact, the key word *ḥērem* is

---

71. Berg, *Book of Esther*, 67.

72. See Berlin, *Esther*, xxxviii. See also Berlin, *Esther*, 85.

73. Wolfe, *Ruth, Esther*, 113.

74. So rightly Bush, *Ruth, Esther*, 476.

entirely lacking from this scene,[75] yet it is found all throughout 1 Samuel 15 (see 1 Sam 15:3, 8–9, 15, 18, 20–21).

Third and most importantly—though scholars have overlooked this point—Esther received the estate of Haman (Esth 8:1, 7) and then gave the estate to Mordecai (8:2). This "estate" would have included all of the property of Haman.[76] If this is not "taking the plunder" I do not know what is. Tragically, then, rather than reversing the failures of King Saul, Esther and Mordecai fall right into the same trap. It was "the Jews" who did not take the plunder (9:10, 15–16), but their leaders took their share (8:1–2, 7) and encouraged them to do likewise (8:10–11). The Jews forsook the plunder of the nations; Esther and Mordecai took the plunder of the "Amalekites."

So then, the refusal to take plunder neither shows that Esther 9 is a "holy war" nor does it show that King Saul's failures were reversed. It may even be the case, as Waltke mentions, that in this context taking plunder from their enemies would have been helpful in restoring and rebuilding the grandeur of the temple.[77] Yet of course, the Jews in the story show no concern for Jerusalem in general, let alone the temple of God (see pp. 17–19 from chapter 1).

Ironic Role Reversals

Some also point to Esther 8:17b as corroborating the notion of "holy war" since it appears to speak of the enemies of the Jews converting to Judaism— "And many people of other nationalities became Jews because fear of the Jews had seized them." The interpretation that this refers to conversion is fairly common.[78] Joyce Baldwin finds this to be a reference to appropriation of religion, claiming, "The religion of the Jews had evidently become a separate issue from that of race."[79] David Firth favors the view that "some form of conversion is described" and that "the dread could include a sense of religious awe."[80] He notes further that the fear of the Jews was a "desacralised

---

75. Craig, *Reading Esther*, 126.

76. De Troyer, *End of the Alpha Text*, 92.

77. Waltke and Yu, *Old Testament Theology*, 768.

78. Fuerst, *Books of Ruth, Esther*, 80; Paton, *Critical and Exegetical Commentary*, 95, 281; Clines, *Esther Scroll*, 28.

79. Baldwin, *Esther*, 99.

80. Firth, *Message of Esther*, 119.

reference to God."[81] Others take this "fear" to be religious awe as well.[82] Yet there is no reason to understand "fear" in this way.[83] There are, of course, examples of divinely inspired fear in the Old Testament (e.g., Josh 2:9–11, 24; 5:1), but this is not one of them. For one, the text makes no mention of the fear of Israel's God or that God caused the fear to come upon them. Most importantly, though, the real problem is that the starting point of this discussion—interpreting "becoming Jews" as conversion—is misguided.

If 8:17 contained a reference to conversion then we would have a clear example of Jewish "religion" in the story of Esther. However, this interpretation is unlikely. The verb in question is in the *Hithpael* stem (*mityahădîm*), which means that it likely carries the connotation of "esteeming or presenting oneself in a state, sometimes with regard to the question of truthfulness," which would then provide us with the possible rendering "pretended to be Jews" in this context.[84] Thus, 8:17 need not be taken as a reference to *religious* change. In the light of this, Adele Berlin renders the verb as "they identified themselves with the Jews," meaning that the Gentiles sided with the Jews in relation to the upcoming battle.[85] Essentially, then, we see here something highly ironic; non-Jews pretending to be Jewish in 8:17 parallels Esther pretending to be a Gentile (see 2:10, 20).[86] In fact, the irony goes deeper; 8:17 shows further how the persecuted become the persecutors and vice versa.[87]

This ironic twist is apparent from the very fact that Mordecai's counter-edict in 8:11 was intended as a response to Haman's edict (3:13), utilizing the same basic terms. See the figure below, where I have utilized the NRSV for reasons that will become clear momentarily:

81. Ibid., 123.

82. Laniak, *Shame and Honor*, 133–34; Clines, *Esther Scroll*, 41.

83. Rightly Fox, *Character and Ideology*, 105; *idem, Redaction of the Books of Esther*, 112; De Troyer, *End of the Alpha Text*, 168.

84. Waltke and O'Connor, *Introduction to Biblical Hebrew Syntax*, 431 (§26.2f.) provides this category for *Hithpael* and offers Esther 8:17 as a possible example. Bush (*Ruth, Esther*, 448) prefers the ambiguous translation, "professed themselves to be Jews."

85. Berlin, *Esther*, 80.

86. So rightly Levenson, *Esther*, 117.

87. So also Klaassen, "Persian/Jew/Jew/Persian," 25.

Haman's Edict (Esther 3:13; NRSV)	Mordecai's Counter-Edict (Esther 8:11; NRSV)
Letters were sent by couriers to all the king's provinces, giving orders to *destroy, to kill, and to annihilate* all Jews, young and old, *women and children*, in one day, the thirteenth of Adar, and *to plunder their goods.*	By these letters the king allowed the Jews who were in every city to assemble and defend their lives, *to destroy, to kill, and to annihilate* any armed force of any people or province that might attack them, with their *children and women*, and *to plunder their goods.*

From a quick comparison of these two edicts we can see that they essentially mirror each other. As summaries of edicts, and not the verbatim content, this accounts for the differences. This means that a basic "tit for tat" approach was to be taken, including the attack of women and children. However, some have thought that the "women and children" in question do not refer to their enemies, but their own women and children. Note J. G. McConville's arguments:

> The words "with their children and women" are important here. Scholars are divided on the question whether this means that the Jews might destroy the women and the children of the peoples who took up arms against them, or whether it means that they might destroy those who took up arms against *them* (i.e., the Jews) along with *their* (i.e. the Jews') women and children. Since the only legitimate target in view is actually "armed forces"—which, as such, do not *have* women and children—the latter interpretation is to be preferred. The decree can then be understood purely as a defensive measure, envisaging no more force than was necessary in order to neutralize the first decree.[88]

This is how the NIV renders the verse and a few others have followed.[89] However, most scholars interpret "women and children" as a reference to the women and children of those who will attack the Jews.[90] Thus, the killing of women and children was permitted by Mordecai's decree. We are not told if the Jews did kill women and children, and perhaps we can infer that, just like they did not take the plunder that they were entitled to by

88. McConville, *Ezra, Nehemiah, and Esther*, 189 (emphasis original).

89. Vos, *Ezra, Nehemiah, and Esther*, 179; Baldwin, *Esther*, 98; Gordis, "Studies in the Esther Narrative," 49–53.

90. So Berlin, *Esther*, 77; Levenson, *Esther*, 110–11; Jobes, *Esther*, 180–81; Bush, *Ruth, Esther*, 447; Fox, *Character and Ideology*, 100; Paton, *Critical and Exegetical Commentary*, 274.

the decree, they did not harm innocent bystanders either. Yet the point to make here is not what the Jews did with the edict but rather that the edict itself points toward the reversal of roles, the persecuted have become the persecutors.

This depiction of ironic reversal is absent from the popular understanding of the story, especially as expressed in the films, cartoons, and novels. But one film in particular strives to make this point clear. In *Exile: Esther* (1986) the Israeli director Amos Gitai was concerned to show "how people who are persecuted can become new persecutors."[91] At the end of the film, Esther's request for a second day of fighting is narrated as Mordecai ominously stares into the camera. In this final sequence, Mordecai is clothed in the same dark outfit that Haman wore throughout the film to make the symbolism of reversal clear. Various sets of the film were modern-day ruins in Israel, which provides a chilling ethos and conflates the conflicts of the past with those of the present. During the scene in which Haman is executed the camera pans across the street and lingers over a mosque while cars drive by and curious onlookers try to figure out what the film crew is up to. The conflation of the modern with the ancient is striking. Just before the credits, the film concludes with each of the actors telling their own personal stories of displacement and exile, as a further example of the conflation. The most intriguing aspect of this portion of the film is that the actor who played Mordecai, Mohammed Bakri, explains that he is actually a Palestinian. He speaks candidly about his intentions in making this film and his feelings about Mordecai:

> After all he had seen, Mordecai forgot what he was fighting for. He wanted to protect his people? Well, he did but he forgot that it was a war of survival. Suddenly the war of survival turned into a cruel and bloody war. A war without justification or end. This is where I see a parallel between today and the past. And that's why I'm angry, and I hate Mordecai. You and I are making this film hoping to prevent such slaughter. Neither of us wants to see the cycle of revenge continue. But it does. And we are both furious, and express our fury in this film.[92]

Bakri's comments are unsettling, and provide a very different perspective than the cute and clean version of the Esther story that many are used to.

---

91. As Gitai explains in the special featurette, "Amos Gitai: Images of Exile," on the DVD.

92. The English text here was taken from the closed captioning subtitles.

Yet the text of Esther points us toward the same basic conclusion as the filmmakers; by the end of the story Esther and Mordecai look far more like Haman than we had probably imagined. This, I think, is most clear in the fact that Esther "one ups" Haman, so to speak, by requesting for Haman's ten (dead) sons to be impaled[93] and asking for a second day of fighting instead of just one (9:13). Some, however, have attempted to minimize the vindictive image of Esther that emerges here. One author suggested that Esther requests a second day of fighting because she had "heard of a Persian plot to attack the Jews on the following day as well."[94] Another suggests that somehow Esther displays "wisdom" in her military strategy.[95] Against charges of cruelty, James Hamilton regards the violence at the end of Esther as part of a typological fulfillment of Genesis 3:16 where it was promised that the seed of the woman would crush the head of the serpent. He states, "The center of the theology of Esther is that God glorifies himself by saving his people through the judgment visited upon their enemies."[96] Hamilton is to be commended for trying to make sense of Esther within his biblical-theological framework of "salvation through judgment." However, I do not regard his interpretation of Esther in this framework to be justified. It seems like the material from Esther has been forced to fit his theological grid.

The second day of battle, therefore, is best read as "literally, overkill."[97] Haman's edict was only intended for a single day and Mordecai's counter-edict had only permitted a single day of fighting—the thirteenth of Adar. Thus, any construal of the Jews merely defending themselves in Esther 9 is seen to be misguided. As Bernhard Anderson notes, the Jews in the story do not appear to be "essentially different from the heathen."[98] He concludes further, "[Mordecai] proves to be the worthy successor of Haman."[99] In fact, in the light of the Talmud's comments on how Purim should be celebrated—a person celebrating Purim should drink to the point that "cursed be Haman" and "blessed be Mordecai" are indistinguishable

93. Impaling the dead was an obvious way to bring shame upon someone (see Deut 21:22–23; Josh 8:29; 10:25–27; 1 Sam 31:10; 2 Sam 4:12).

94. Pfeiffer, *Wycliffe Bible Commentary*, 456.

95. Bechtel, *Esther*, 79.

96. Hamilton, *God's Glory in Salvation through Judgment*, 322.

97. So Fox, *Character and Ideology*, 203.

98. B. Anderson, "Place of the Book of Esther," 41.

99. Ibid., 39.

(*b. Meg.* 7b)—Matthew Klaassen notes how this ironic reversal can be seen in the celebration of Purim itself, "that the Jews have now adopted a festival of drunkenness just as the Persians had at the beginning of the story shows the extent to which the Jews have become Persian."[100]

We might look at the origin of Purim (9:20–32), however—which is a central celebration in the liturgical calendar of the Jews—as demonstrating the story's religious significance.[101] Perhaps this may be seen as a way of vindicating the characters from all the negativity that we have seen in Esther 9? It seems best to conclude that the means toward relief and deliverance was not morally appropriate, yet this does not nullify the importance of the deliverance that the Jews experienced. Haman had decreed to kill every Jew in all the provinces after all (3:13). Certainly, the celebration of the existence of a people in the face of such conflict would be expected. We should resist, however, the urge to alter the story because of its connection to Purim. Note the words of Brevard Childs, "The original story of the persecution and rescue of the Jews is retained as normative scripture along with its intrigue, brutality, nationalism, and secularity, but the story has been given a new theological interpretation within the worship of Israel."[102] He explains further, and I cite him in full:

> The manner of the celebration in all its original "secularity" is unchanged, but the object of the hilarity is redefined. All Israel shares in the joy of rest and relief which is dramatized by the giving of gifts, especially to the poor. It is a time to remember by hearing again the story of Purim. The effect of the reshaping of the festival is not to make a secular festival into a religious one, but to interpret the meaning of Purim in all its secularity in the context of Israel's existence, which is religious. The very language by which the festival is now regulated as the "appointed seasons", "gifts to the poor," "rest from enemies," "remembrance throughout every generation . . . for ever," draws Purim within the orbit of Israel's religious traditions. The canonical shape does not attempt to eliminate offensive elements in the original story (e.g., 9.13), but it does carefully define what the effect of the story is to be on successive generations.[103]

100. Klaassen, "Persian/Jew/Jew/Persian," 24.

101. So Levenson (*Esther*, 18) asserts, "If secularity be defined as the absence of mention of the Deity or of religious institutions, then we must say that at no point in its compositional history was the book of Esther secular."

102. Childs, *Introduction to the Old Testament*, 604.

103. Ibid., 604–5.

So there is indeed a profound deliverance depicted in this text, and the Festival of Purim was designed to commemorate this, but the important point is this: *the story of Esther is a self-critical reflection on deliverance.*[104] The deliverance of the Jews is worth celebrating, but this does not mean that Esther and Mordecai were exemplars. Far from it.

Conclusion & Summary

In this chapter I have suggested that there are no positive examples of Jewish devotion, faith, or piety in the story of Esther. Even if the previous chapter (*Esther & the Compromise*), with its negative portrayal of the characters, were omitted from our study we still would have no reason to conclude that our characters had religious convictions or intuitions. This renders the thesis of Humphreys to be a severe misreading—"[Esther] present[s] a style of life for the diaspora Jew which affirms most strongly that at one and the same time the Jew can remain loyal to his heritage and God and yet can live a creative, rewarding, and fulfilled life precisely within a foreign setting."[105] There is nothing in the text that warrants any such conclusion about loyalty to God or their ancestral faith in this foreign setting. In fact, in this chapter we have seen precisely the opposite.

There is, however, one person in the story who expresses the sort of covenantal theology that we might expect from our characters. Zeresh, the wife of Haman, confidently asserts that if Mordecai "is of Jewish origin" (lit., "from the seed of the Jews") Haman will surely fall before him (6:13). Yet why do we not read of this confidence from any of the Jews in the story? Why is it a Gentile who expresses the theology of "offspring" and "seed" that evokes the covenantal promises made to Abraham and David?[106] Just as Vashti was seen as to be a foil for Esther's participation in the sexual compe-

---

104. So also Klaassen, "Persian/Jew/Jew/Persian," 25.

105. Humphreys, "Life-Style for Diaspora," 233. Crawford ("Esther," 136) suggests similarly, though with less of an emphasis on Esther as an exemplary *religious* model, "[Esther] serves as the role model for all diaspora Jews who find themselves in a minority status. This, then, is the original purpose of the book: to acquaint the Jews in the Eastern Diaspora with a mode of conduct that will enable them to attain security and to lead happy and productive lives. Esther the queen, by her deeds and in her character, typifies this mode of life." If this was indeed the author's purpose, does that mean that the author wants his audience to suppress their religious convictions and their God-ordained "separated-ness" in order to flourish? This seems like a very unlikely purpose for the book.

106. Rightly Firth, *Message of Esther*, 98. See Gen 12:1–3; 2 Sam 7:1–17.

tition and eventual pagan marriage, so too another Gentile woman (Zeresh) functions as a critique of the covenantal theology of the Jews. There is no apparent awareness among the Jews of any covenantal obligations to Israel's God (e.g., the Mosaic law), or any sense of trust in the God who keeps his covenantal promises to Abraham and David, or any sense of belief that the God of the exodus could once again provide deliverance. Rather, we have seen the covenantal laws broken, and the covenantal promises ignored.

On the whole, we have not been given any reason to regard either Esther or Mordecai as exemplars of Jewish faith, piety, or devotion. Thus, I agree with the conclusion of Bruce Waltke regarding the author of Esther, "His lack of prayer, praise, and piety silently drives home his message: these are nominal Jews, not true Israel."[107] What we will see in the next chapter, however, is that many were uncomfortable with this fact and sought to change it.

---

107. Waltke and Yu, *Old Testament Theology*, 768.

3

Esther & the Cover-Up

It has been argued thus far that there are elements in the story of Esther that pious Jews from the post-exilic period would have found troublesome, and furthermore, that there were no examples that we could point to in an effort to demonstrate that Esther and Mordecai were, in the end, somehow pious themselves. The portrait of the Jewish characters that we are left with is one of assimilation and secularization.

In rounding out part 1 of this study, where the focus has been on the interpretation of the text, we now turn to the final issue that demonstrates the moral and religious deficiencies of the story—the expansive translations of the book into Greek and Aramaic. The tale of Esther that we have just explored underwent remarkable changes, apparently from the very start. In this chapter we will look at both the Greek and the Aramaic expansions on the Hebrew story to see how some of the earliest interpreters of the Esther story tried to make it more palatable, religious, and "biblical."[1] The study will begin by focusing on the two Greek translations of Esther before transitioning into the two Aramaic translations. The goal of this chapter is not to point out every little difference between the translations (and there are quite a lot), but to specifically make mention of the various religious expansions and modifications of the story. After looking at the translations, the religious expansions of these ancient texts will be seen in relation to contemporary retellings of the Esther story, such as the films, cartoons, and romance novels. What we will see is that interpreters, both ancient and

---

1. Note the words of Clines in this regard, "The primary effect of the LXX expansions as a whole is, I would suggest, to *assimilate the book of Esther to a scriptural norm*, especially as found in Ezra, Nehemiah, and Daniel" (*Esther Scroll*, 169; emphasis original).

modern, have tried to adjust the story. Just like Esther as a character, the story of Esther seems to have undergone its own cosmetic enhancements, though this cover-up conceals far more blemishes than twelve months in ancient Persia ever could.

The Greek Translations

There are two ancient Greek translations of the story of Esther. The more well-known Greek translation comes from the collection commonly known as the Septuagint, designated by the Latin abbreviation for "seventy," LXX, because of a popular legend that seventy-two scholars completed the Greek translation of the Torah in seventy-two days (*Letter of Aristeas* 50, 307). Under differing circumstances, each of the books of the Old Testament were translated into Greek within the third to the first centuries BCE.[2] Thus, the Septuagint version of Esther was likely translated within that time. The other Greek translation of the Esther story, known as the Alpha Text (designated AT), is preserved in only four medieval manuscripts.[3]

Yet the existence of two Greek traditions raises several problems for the study of Esther. For instance, how do we know which Greek translation came first? Also, were these translations independent of each other or was one possibly correcting the other? To shake things up even further, is it possible that one of these traditions predates the Hebrew version? These issues are significant and can have a dramatic impact on how one interprets the text and understands the origin of the Esther story. For these issues the reader is directed to the appendix at the end of this book, which should be consulted in conjunction with this chapter. The appendix primarily explains why I think that all religious adjustments to Esther are secondary, and that the Hebrew version that we have, in all its secularity, best reflects the primitive story. You may find yourself content with this summary, but if you wish to see how I defend such a position please check the appendix. Regardless of whether or not one understands every little detail about the two Greek translations of Esther, we will primarily want to consider the intentions of those who added to the text.

---

2. Jobes and Silva, *Invitation to the Septuagint*, 31–32. The Septuagint also includes the so-called "apocryphal" books.

3. The manuscripts are numbered 19, 93, 108, and 319, each dating from the 10th to the 13th century. See Fox, *Redaction of the Books of Esther*, 10; Jobes, *Alpha-Text of Esther*, 2–3.

And we are not talking about slight adjustments! The LXX of the Esther story actually adds 107 verses overall to the Hebrew story, which has 167 verses.[4] These new verses are primarily clumped into six major additions, called the Additions to Esther. The additions are found throughout the narrative and are often labeled A through F, though sometimes as chapters 11 through 16. The reason for the odd numbering system in the latter designation is because the Western church father Jerome, who translated the Bible into Latin (i.e., the Vulgate), noticed that there were no Hebrew manuscripts that contained the additional sections of the Greek manuscripts. So for his Latin translation he excised each additional section from its narratival context and placed them at the end of the story after Esther 10:3 (hence, 11–16).[5] For this study I will refer to both sets of references. The AT contains all six additions found in the LXX, but because the AT is about twenty percent shorter than the LXX,[6] it has its own unique numbering system for versification.

To make all of this a little easier to understand it may be helpful to categorize the six additions into three sets of two. Additions A and F bookend the story with Mordecai's dream (Addition A) prior to Esther 1 and the interpretation of the dream (Addition F) after Esther 10:3, Additions B and E provide the specifics for Haman's edict and Mordecai's counter-edict respectively, and Additions C and D heighten the tension and drama of the events leading up to and including Esther's petition to the king.

The procedure of this section will be to survey the text according to the chronology of the LXX, utilizing it as the main launching point for discussion with supplemental comments provided on the AT when its reading is unique.[7] In so doing I will make note of each of the six major additions as well as important alterations within the body of the text in order to see the explicit theology of the Greek translations.[8]

4. Noted in Baldwin, *Esther*, 45. Some of the six Additions were possibly Semitic in origin (so Clines, *Esther Scroll*, 69; Law, *When God Spoke Greek*, 61–63; R. Martin, "Syntax Criticism of the LXX Additions," 65–72; C. Moore, "On the Origins of the LXX Additions," 382–93), yet there are no Semitic sources of Esther that contain these additions, so they are only attested in antiquity in Greek texts (see Jobes, *Alpha-Text of Esther*, 162; Jobes and Silva, *Invitation to the Septuagint*, 295; C. Moore, *Daniel, Esther, and Jeremiah*, 153–54).

5. C. Moore, *Daniel, Esther, and Jeremiah*, 154.

6. See Jobes, *Alpha-Text of Esther*, 147.

7. All citations of the AT are taken from Clines's English translation in *Esther Scroll*, 216–47.

8. For the LXX I will utilize the English translation provided by the NRSV.

Addition A (Esther 11:2—12:6)

Addition A precedes the traditional narrative of Esther and describes a vision that Mordecai received. This unique introduction is not mentioned anywhere else in the Greek narrative, but does find further comment in the new epilogue of the story (Addition F) where the dream is interpreted.

Within the dream, Mordecai receives a vision of two large dragons "ready to fight" (A 11:6), all the nations prepared to battle alongside the two dragons.[9] The righteous nation that was opposed by one of the dragons feared their survival and called out to God. Because of their prayers, God caused a "tiny spring" to become "a great river" that brought about the downfall of the unjust (A 11:10–11). This opening vision is no doubt meant to show that the story of Esther should be understood from within the life of faith and the providence of God.

When Mordecai awoke from his dream he overheard that there would be an attack against the king. After warning the king, the two guilty chamberlains were executed (A 12:1–3) and Mordecai was given gifts for his service (A 12:5). In response to this we find that Haman was displeased with the promotion of Mordecai and began to resent both him and his people (A 12:6). Thus, we are presented with hostility against the Jews, and specifically the conflict with Haman, before the traditional Esther material begins. This has the effect of removing any element of compromise from Esther's role in the competition to replace Vashti and gives Esther a newfound sense of purpose—to save her people.

Esther 2:20 LXX

In between Addition A and Addition B there is a significant change in the body of the text at Esther 2:20 (LXX). We saw in chapter 1 of this study how this verse pointed to the fact that Esther had been keeping her heritage a secret long before she had entered the royal competition (see p. 33). However, note the reading in the LXX, "Esther had not disclosed her country—such were the instructions of Mordecai; but she was to fear God and keep his

---

9. The cosmic nature of the opposition between the two dragons in Additions A and F appears to be influenced by Jewish Apocalypticism. See Moore, *Daniel, Esther, and Jeremiah*, 181. The addition of apocalyptic material, although unrelated to the original intentions of Esther, coheres with the ethos of apocalyptic more broadly, which is to provide a covenantal hope in the midst of unmet covenantal expectations aggravated by suffering and/or persecution. See my forthcoming, "Suffering and Covenantal Hope."

laws, just as she had done when she was with him. So Esther did not change her mode of life" (Esth 2:20 LXX). This text not only communicates the opposite message of what I argued for earlier, but also inserts the notion of "fearing God" and implicitly refers to the Mosaic law. The AT, however, makes no mention of Esther hiding her identity or being commanded to do so. Rather, we simply read that Mordecai "was faithfully bringing up" Esther (Esth 3:7 AT).

Addition B (Esther 13:1–7)

The purpose of Addition B is to disclose the contents of the letter referenced in Esther 3:13, which the Hebrew story (Masoretic Text; hereafter MT) does not provide. Essentially, the letter states that the Jews were antagonistic to society.

Esther 4:8 LXX

Another significant change within the body of the text is at Esther 4:8 (LXX), where Mordecai tries to convince Esther to go before the king. In the LXX the Greek expands upon the Hebrew in explicitly including prayer—"Call upon the Lord; then speak to the king in our behalf, and save us from death."

Esther 4:14, 16 MT (Esther 5:8, 11 AT)

Rather than speak nebulously of "another place" in Esther 4:14, the AT reads, "If you neglect to help your people, then God will be their help and salvation" (Esth 5:8 AT). The historian Josephus, who includes his own retelling of the Esther story, likewise records Mordecai saying, "There would certainly arise help to them from God some other way" (Ant. 11.6.7). No doubt Josephus and the AT reflect an intentional explanation of what "from another place" means. Interestingly, though, the AT omits any reference to fasting from this scene but offers more religiously obvious material: "Proclaim a service of worship and pray earnestly to God" (Esth 5:11 AT).[10]

---

10. Similarly, some of the popular retellings of Esther replace fasting with more explicit religious imagery. In Norah Lofts's novel, Esther's message to Mordecai reads, "You gather the Jews together and pray." See Lofts, Esther, 119.

Addition C (Esther 13:8—14:19)

A prayer of Mordecai is inserted after Esther consents to go to the king un-summoned (Esth 4:17 MT). This addition is the most theologically significant for the Greek versions of Esther. As Karen Jobes asserts, "The overall effect of Addition C . . . draws the Esther story from the periphery into the mainstream tradition of the Pentateuch."[11] Some of the major emphases of Mordecai's prayer include: God's role as creator and king, his sovereignty, omnipotence, omniscience, and his glory. Mordecai's decision not to bow to Haman is given a pietistic gloss, "But I did this so that I might not set human glory above the glory of God, and I will not bow down to anyone but you, who are my Lord" (C 13:14).[12] God's covenant with Israel is also stressed. This is seen through references to Abraham (C 13:15) and the exodus (C 13:16); the reference to the exodus is especially significant in the light of the fact that the Jews do not recognize that Haman's edict was issued on the first day of Passover![13] Israel is referred to as the Lord's people—his "portion" (C 13:16) and "inheritance" (C 13:15, 17).

Following Mordecai's prayer is a prayer from Esther (C 14:1–19). Esther removed her attractive garments and put on clothes of lament, placing ashes and dung upon her head (C 14:2); however, in the Hebrew story she does not appropriate the clothes of lament. The primary concern of the prayer is to ask for strength and courage as she prepares to visit the king unannounced. In Esther's prayer, God is Israel's king (C 14:3); he is "King of the gods and Master of all dominion" (C 14:12). Israel's covenantal relationship with God is also a major aspect of her prayer. Esther reminds the Lord that he chose Israel and their fathers as an "everlasting inheritance" (C 14:5). The Lord is called "Lord God of Abraham" (C 14:18). Reference is made to God's house, the temple, and the altar (C 14:9). Their current state of distress is interpreted covenantally as a curse due to their idolatry (C 14:6–10). Further, Esther notes that she despises the bed of the uncircumcised and foreigners (C 14:15). She also presents herself as one who is merely performing a duty when acting as queen and that deep down she loathes and despises her position like a menstrual rag (C 14:16). The overall effect of both of these prayers is to remove the tension regarding Esther's

---

11. Jobes, *Alpha-Text of Esther*, 179–80.

12. Josephus describes his refusal to bow similarly, "Mordecai was so wise, and so observant of his own country's laws, that he would not worship the man" (*Ant.*, 11.6.5).

13. See pp. 54–56 of chapter 2.

marriage to a Gentile king, and to show dependence on God in this time of need.

Addition D (Esther 15:1–16)

Whereas the other Additions are lengthy insertions into the story of Esther, Addition D is a little more woven into the fabric of the text, taking Esther 5:1–2 (MT) with its brief description of Esther going before the king, expanding it considerably.[14] It references Esther's prayer, that she called upon the "all-seeing God and Savior" (D 15:2). Furthermore, Addition D notes that ultimately God was providentially in control of the disposition of the king—"God changed the spirit of the king to gentleness" (D 15:8; see also Esth 6:7 AT).[15] It was not until God changed the king's heart that the king ceased from looking at Esther "in fierce anger" which caused her to collapse and faint (D 15:7).[16] Esther explained that she was afraid of the king because he looked "like an angel of God" (D 15:13; see also Esth 6:11 AT). This image of a terrifying king is out of step with the Hebrew story, where we see the king constantly throwing feasts, lavishly treating his guests to wine with "no restrictions" (Esth 1:7–8 MT), and giving gifts "with royal liberality" (Esth 2:18 MT). The image of the king in the Hebrew version is therefore only as scary as a drunken Santa Claus (though that is admittedly terrifying in its own right).

14. 1 Clement 55:6 mentions Esther's courage and humiliation in going before the king, showing dependence on the Greek version of the Esther story, particularly Additions C and D, in saying—"To no less danger did Esther, who was perfect in faith, expose herself, in order that she might deliver the twelve tribes of Israel when they were about to be destroyed. For through her fasting and her humiliation she entreated the all-seeing Master, the God of the ages, and he, seeing the humility of her soul, rescued the people for whose sake she had faced the danger" (see Holmes, *Apostolic Fathers*, 59). In this context the author was comparing Esther with Judith (55:4–5), another Jewish heroine (her story can be found in the Apocrypha). While her people are under siege, Judith devises a plan to overthrow her enemies by using her beauty as well as food to her advantage (just as Esther used her beauty and banquets). Judith, who "feared God" (8:8), was able to entice the general of the enemy army, Holofernes. She stayed overnight, yet she did not eat his food during her covert mission (12:1–4), and later notes that she "did not sin with him" (13:16; see also 16:22). She was able to get him drunk after feasting and then decapitate him (12:10—13:10). In chapter 16 there is a long hymn of thanksgiving that Judith offers to God for her people's victory. And Judith devoted the possessions of Holofernes to God as an offering (16:19).

15. Josephus records similarly that the king changed his mind "as I suppose, by the will of God" (*Ant.*, 11.6.9).

16. See Josephus, *Ant.*, 11.6.9, as well.

Esther 6:1 LXX (AT 7:1)

One of the most significant turning points in the story is when the king "coincidentally" could not sleep the night that Haman was preparing to kill Mordecai. The LXX states that "the Lord took sleep from the king" (Esth 6:1 LXX). Likewise the AT says that "the Mighty one" did this (Esth 7:1 AT). Similarly, Josephus reads, "God laughed to scorn the wicked expectations of Haman" and took away the king's sleep (*Ant.* 11.6.10).[17]

Esther 6:13 LXX

The words of Zeresh, that Haman would fall before Mordecai because he was a Jew (Esth 6:13 MT), is expanded in the Greek—"because the living God is with him."[18]

Esther 8:2 (AT)

When Esther was about to confront Haman during the second banquet with the king, the AT informs the reader that "God gave her courage" (Esth 8:2 AT).

Addition E (Esther 16:1–24)

This Addition provides the contents of Mordecai's counter-edict (between Esther 8:12 and 8:13 MT). It is similar to Addition B, but contains much more theological language. The edict mentions the opponents of the Jews as those who try to escape the "evil-hating justice of God" (E 16:4). An emphasis on the uprightness of the Jews is also found in this edict; it states that the Jews are not criminals, but are governed by "most righteous laws" (E 16:15). As Carey Moore notes, the edict would have resonated well with pious Jews of the diaspora who desired to practice their religion without discrimination.[19] The Jews are said to be "children of the living God, most high, most mighty" (E 16:16). In regards to Haman's sentence to death, the

---

17. Josephus also extols the wisdom of God in bringing about the reversal so that Haman died on the gallows prepared for Mordecai (*Ant.*, 11.6.11).

18. See also Josephus, *Ant.*, 11.6.10; and Esth 7:22 AT.

19. C. Moore, *Daniel, Esther, and Jeremiah*, 238.

edict states that the "God, who rules over all things" has brought about this punishment (E 16:18). Furthermore, the edict states that the "God, who rules over all things" has delivered "his chosen people" (E 16:21).

Esther 8:17 LXX (AT 7:41)

In chapter 2 of this study (*Esther & the Covenant*, see pp. 60–61) we saw that the idea of "becoming Jews" in 8:17 likely refers to Gentiles either pretending to be Jewish or positionally aligning themselves with the Jews to avoid harm. Intriguingly, the ambiguity of the passage was taken in two different yet similar ways within the two Greek traditions. Both regard this as a reference to "circumcision" specifically (something missing from the Hebrew text), though in the LXX it is the Gentiles who receive circumcision (Esth 8:17 LXX)[20] and in the AT the Jews circumcise themselves![21]

Esther 8:34 AT

When Mordecai writes that Purim is to be celebrated annually in commemoration of their deliverance, it is further expanded so that they are to "keep festival to God."

Addition F (Esther 10:4—11:1)

After the traditional Esther story concludes at 10:3, Addition F provides the explanation for the dream recorded in Addition A. Mordecai remembers his dream and concludes, "These things have come from God" (F 10:4). In the LXX, the river represents Esther (F 10:6), the two dragons represent Haman and Mordecai (F 10:7) and the nations represent all those opposed to Israel (F 10:8).[22] Then, of course, there is Israel, whom Mordecai states "cried out to God and was saved" (F 10:9). He concludes again that the Lord has saved and rescued his people by performing signs and wonders unlike

---

20. So also Josephus, *Ant.*, 11.6.13.

21. No doubt this was due to taking the *Hithpael* stem of the verb as reflexive.

22. Yet in the AT the representations are slightly different. There the river represents the enemies of the Jews (AT F:54). This has lead Moore to conclude that Additions A and F circulated independently for a while (see C. Moore, *Daniel, Esther, and Jeremiah*, 248–49). Jobes doubts this and suggests instead that Additions A and F represent the last redactional strata of the Greek story of Esther. See Jobes, *Alpha-Text of Esther*, 183–84.

what had ever occurred among pagans (F 10:9). Essentially, the impact of the prologue (Addition A) and epilogue (Addition F) is to subordinate the events of the Esther story to Mordecai's dream, making him "the unambiguous hero of the story" and God as the active participant behind the scenes.[23]

Addition F also contains a final colophon (F 11:1). The colophon was written in the fourth year of the reign of Ptolemy and Cleopatra.[24] It states that a certain Dositheus, who claimed to be a Levitical priest, brought the "Letter about Purim" with his son Ptolemy. The colophon mentions that the book was "authentic" and was translated by a member of the Jerusalem community. Most scholars note that there is no reason to doubt the reliability of this section, which becomes especially valuable for dating purposes.[25]

Since the colophon includes a comment about the translation of Esther being "authentic," it is true that, as Daniel Harrington notes, "the colophon is a witness to ancient suspicions surrounding the book of Esther."[26] I do not believe it is the case, however, as Harrington suggests about Esther LXX as a whole, that "the Greek version makes explicit the implicit theology of the Hebrew text."[27] Does the Hebrew version of Esther really contain an "implicit theology" along the lines that the Greek texts develop? The appeal to "implicit theology" appears to be special pleading. It is, in fact, a chief irony that the Greek versions of Esther exude religious piety and devotion whereas the Hebrew text represents such extreme degrees of assimilation. The irony is because nothing "demonstrates the Hellenization of the Jews . . . more spectacularly than the Greek translation of the Hebrew Scriptures."[28] The evidence from the Greek translations demonstrates that the Hebrew text of Esther was initially conceived to be either ambiguous, and therefore in need of clarification, or theologically bankrupt, and therefore in need of conversion. And as we will now see, so did those who translated Esther into Aramaic.

---

23. So rightly Jobes, *Alpha-Text of Esther*, 184–85.

24. These names were common for regal pairs and so the date of composition was either 114 BCE, 77 BCE, or 48 BCE. See C. Moore, *Daniel, Esther, and Jeremiah*, 250.

25. Baldwin, *Esther*, 47; C. Moore, *Daniel, Esther, and Jeremiah*, 250–52.

26. Harrington, *Invitation to the Apocrypha*, 52.

27. Ibid.

28. Law, *When God Spoke Greek*, 17.

Aramaic Targums

Another intriguing source for seeing how the Esther story developed into something far beyond what it was originally meant to be are the Aramaic Targums from the sixth and seventh centuries CE.[29] Targums are Rabbinic sources that are essentially Aramaic paraphrases of the Hebrew Scriptures. Intriguingly, the book of Esther alone, outside the Torah, has a second independent Targum.[30] This has been explained as a demonstration of the importance of the story of Esther, and indeed this is certainly the case. Yet the existence of two independent and very divergent Targummic traditions likely reflects the ambiguity of Esther.[31] Esther *needed* to be clarified. And so we will look at these two clarifications closely, one at a time.

Targum Rishon

In *Targum Rishon* (hereafter *Tg. R.*) we read that Esther was a descendant of Sarah (*Tg. R.* 1:1), whereas Mordecai is introduced in the original Esther story with negative associations, such as, (a) Shimei, who cursed the line of David, (b) Saul (by implication), the disobedient king who was also the first king, and (c) Jehoiachin, who was one of the last kings of Judah before the Babylonian exile, himself a bad king. Therefore, introducing Esther as a descendant of Sarah was probably meant to counter the negative associations that we saw in chapter 1 (see pp. 19–22).

For the opening chapter of Esther, *Tg. R.* mentions that the utensils from the Jerusalem temple were being used at the king's party (*Tg. R.* 1:7; likely recalling Dan 5:2), although several texts state that the temple utensils were returned when Cyrus permitted the Jews to return and rebuild the temple (Ezra 1:7–11; 5:13–15). *Tg. R.* also makes a note of something left ambiguous from the Hebrew, that Mordecai and his close associates were not at this grand party (*Tg. R.* 1:7). Instead, Mordecai was praying and fasting during this event (*Tg. R.* 1:10). We are also told that one of the chief eunuchs from the original scene, Memuchan, is actually Haman (*Tg. R.* 1:16; see also *b. Meg.* 12b).[32] Just as we saw earlier (see p. 71), several interpreters

---

29. All of citations of the Targums are from Grossfeld, *Two Targums of Esther*.

30. Paton, *Critical and Exegetical Commentary*, 21.

31. Likewise, the only midrashic explanation of an entire biblical book in the Talmud is Esther (*b. Meg.* 10b–17a). Perhaps this was for similar reasons. See Berlin, *Esther*, liii.

32. In *Targum Sheni*, Memuchan is Daniel rather than Haman (*Tg. S.* 1:16).

tried to insert Haman or general notions of hostility against the Jews prior to the beauty competition. In this context Haman is introduced as "grandson of Agag the evil one" (*Tg. R.* 1:16), exposing the hostility much earlier than the Hebrew story (see Esth 3:6).

When chapter 2 begins we are properly introduced to Mordecai as "a pious man who prayed before God for his people," and, in an attempt to distance his name from Marduk no doubt, he is said to be called Mordecai because "he was comparable to pure myrrh" (*Tg. R.* 2:5).[33] Mordecai's relationship to Shimei is also given an interesting explanation. Shimei originally cursed David, as noted before, and was allowed to live for some time afterward but was put to death by Solomon several years later. The text says that the reason Shimei was allowed to live for so long was because David foresaw the birth of Esther and Mordecai (*Tg. R.* 2:5; see also *Targum Sheni* 2:5).

After Esther wins the competition, the Targum expands greatly on the idea that Esther kept her Jewish heritage a secret in 2:20:

> *Sabbaths and Festivals she would observe; during the days of separation she watched herself,* cooked dishes and wine of the nations she did not taste, and all the religious precepts which the women of the House of Israel were commanded, she observed by order of Mordecai, just as she observed (them) when she grew up with him. (*Tg. R.* 2:20; original italics meant to represent expansions)

This is an interesting expansion because the text was originally communicating that she had been in the habit of concealing her Jewish heritage for some time,[34] and this text not only communicates the opposite of that, but also imports a strong depiction of piety and devotion.

Mordecai's refusal to bow to Haman is also given an interesting spin. Haman had an image of a god placed on his chest and so if Mordecai bowed down to him it would have been idolatrous (*Tg. R.* 3:2). This similarly infuriated Haman and when he left to cast lots in order to determine when he would attempt to kill all the Jews, a divine voice spoke a word of comfort to Israel: "If you turn about through repentance, then the lot will fall on him instead of you" (*Tg. R.* 3:7). When Haman described to the king how different the Jewish people were from the rest, the text is expanded to include, "Our bread and our cooked dishes they do not eat, our wine they do not drink" (*Tg. R.* 3:8).

33. For Mordecai's name in relation to Marduk, see pp. 22–25.

34. See p. 33 of chapter 1.

Of course, we have seen how some interpreters regard Esther 4 as a scene of repentance.[35] Though in order for Esther 4 to have this significance there must be something for which the people repent. In *Tg. R.* we are introduced to a pious Esther and Mordecai, so why the need to repent? The answer given is that the Jews had participated in the king's feast from Esther 1 (*Tg. R.* 4:1). When Mordecai tells Esther to go before the king he tells her that deliverance will come from "the Lord of the Universe" (*Tg. R.* 4:14) and so when Esther calls a fast she requests that the Jews "pray before the Lord of the Universe" (*Tg. R.* 4:16). Whereas we noted that this fast begins on the first day of Passover even though the characters in the story show no recognition of this, *Tg. R.* states that the fast "transgressed the joy of the festival of Passover" (*Tg. R.* 4:17).

Before Esther goes before the king we are reminded that it was "the third day of Passover" and before she enters the king's gate "the spirit of the Holy One rested upon her; and she proceeded to pray" (*Tg. R.* 5:1). The placement of the prayer at this point in the story is similar to Addition D in the Greek translations. The content, however, is quite different, though there is a similar sensibility regarding the disdain for her current office. In a rather amusing moment, Esther says in her prayer:

> [Haman] *wanted* [the king] *to marry his daughter; thus when the maidens were assembled into the custody of Hegai, Haman's daughter was there, and then it was determined from Heaven that each day she became defiled with excrement and with urine; her mouth also smelled exceedingly offensive, whereupon they hurried her out. For this reason it fell upon me to be married to him.* (*Tg. R.* 5:1)

Talk about providence! When the king offers Esther up to half of his kingdom he specifically mentions that rebuilding the temple in Jerusalem is not an option (*Tg. R.* 5:3). This seemingly random statement, absent from the Hebrew story, is likely meant to shed a positive light on Esther. It was probably thought that a good Jew, given the generous offer of the king, would have chosen to restore the temple. Esther is not given the opportunity to show her affection for Jerusalem and for the temple, but surely a pious Jew like Esther would have requested such if she had the opportunity, right?

After the downfall of Haman, the Jews are shown studying the law, circumcising their children, and putting phylacteries on their head (*Tg. R.* 8:16). And the non-Jews were converting (*Tg. R.* 8:17).

35. See pp. 41–42 of chapter 2.

When the thirteenth of Adar came and the Jews defeated their enemies, it is specifically stated that all those killed in Susa were "from the house of Amalek" (*Tg. R.* 9:6) and all those in the provinces as well (*Tg. R.* 9:16–18). *Tg. R.* also omits the second day of fighting (*Tg. R.* 9:13). In doing such things the intent appears to make the fighting more palatable.

Targum Sheni

Targum Sheni (hereafter *Tg. S.*) is the second Targum on Esther. Similar to *Tg. R.*, we see the wealth of the Jerusalem temple at the feast recorded in Esther 1 (*Tg. S.* 1:3–4). The Targum states that Mordecai went back to Jerusalem to help with the temple after initially being exiled but was then sent into exile again for a second time (*Tg. S.* 2:6). This was given as a way to explain why such a pious Jew would remain so far away from Jerusalem by his own volition.

When Mordecai heard of the decree for the virgins to be brought to the king, he attempted to hide Esther and only succumbed after the king issued a warning that all those trying to hide will be executed (*Tg. S.* 2:8). After Esther was brought to the king's palace, she is depicted as giving her gifts to her handmaidens because she did not want to "taste from the wine of the king's palace" (*Tg. S.* 2:9). Although Haman is not introduced before the king's competition, Mordecai suspected that the king may want to destroy the Jews, and so we find hostility toward the Jews before Esther participated in the competition (*Tg. S.* 2:10). When Haman was promoted, instead of bowing down to him, Mordecai declared, "I only bow down to the ever-existing God who is One in heaven" and he continued a doxology in which he extolled God for his handiwork in creation (*Tg. S.* 3:3; see also *Tg. S.* 6:1).

After the decree to kill the Jews had been declared, Mordecai summoned the Jews to repent and to consider the actions of the people of Nineveh during the time of Jonah (*Tg. S.* 4:1). In the Hebrew version, when Mordecai and Esther discussed whether or not she should go before the king, Esther mentioned that she had not seen the king for thirty days. In *Tg. S.* this is clarified so that actually Esther had been praying the whole time that she would not be summoned to go before the king and thus sin with him (*Tg. S.* 4:11). Mordecai's reference to "from another place" in the Hebrew is expanded to "their Holy One and Redeemer" (*Tg. S.* 4:14). Instead of confining herself to imminent death in 4:16, Esther expressed confidence in the afterlife ("the world to come"; *Tg. S.* 4:16). She also prays before she goes before the king (*Tg. S.* 5:1) as in Addition D. In this prayer she recalls God's preservation of Daniel's three friends in the fiery furnace and Daniel himself in the lion's den (*Tg. S.* 5:1). At the end, when the Jews are victorious there is a doxology of praise for God's deliverance in bringing about the defeat of Haman (*Tg. S.* 8:15), something surprisingly absent from the Hebrew version.

Popular Versions

After looking at the ancient translations of the Esther story we can see that from very early on interpreters were changing the story. But has anything really changed? What about the versions of the story that we tell to others? What about the versions of the story that we preach on Sundays, discuss in Bible studies, watch in films and cartoons, and read in romance novels? An intriguing phenomenon in the reception of Esther is that those who claim to cherish the Hebrew version of the story—who make no use of the expansive texts for personal devotion, and may have never even heard of the Additions to Esther found in the Catholic and Orthodox canons—embrace a version of the Esther story, functionally speaking, that is much more akin to the expansive versions than the Hebrew. As Jo Carruthers notes, "The frequency with which Protestants turn to these 'unauthoritative' (yet ironically more religious) Additions to support their spiritual readings is striking."[36] For many this is no doubt unintentional; but somehow many follow the same unwritten script.

In a few examples from the popular retellings of Esther it appears to be the case that the author/filmmaker was at least somewhat familiar with the expanded versions of Esther. In *One Night with the King* (2006), Esther faints when she appears before the king un-summoned (see Esth 5:1–2), something only recorded in the Greek versions (and no doubt for dramatic effect).

However some popular versions make explicit use of the Greek traditions. In the film, *The Book of Esther* (2013), the opening sequence includes Mordecai having the same dream from Additions A and F in the Greek translations. The key elements are all present, including the earthquakes, the two great dragons that battle alongside the nations, and a little stream becoming a great river. Interestingly, in the director's commentary on the

---

36. Carruthers, *Esther through the Centuries*, 9.

DVD—which includes both the director and the actor who played Esther, Jen Lilley—the director explains that there was some hesitancy in including this scene in the film. I assume this hesitancy was because the dream sequence is not found in the Hebrew version, but Jen Lilley can be heard telling the director that it should have been in the movie since "they talk about it in the actual book of Esther." However, the film shows very little direct dependence on the LXX more broadly and seems to have been intentionally trying to retell the *Hebrew* version of the story, which makes the conversation between the director and Lilley all the more intriguing.

Joan Wolf's *A Reluctant Queen* also contains Mordecai's same dragon dream mentioned in Additions A and F,[37] but her use of the expansive Greek traditions is much more noticeable and apparent. Just as the LXX depicts Esther's struggle with reconciling her position in the pagan palace with her religious convictions, so too in Wolf's novel Esther prays something similar to what can be found in Addition C—"Give me the courage to keep my purity, even though I must live in this unclean place."[38] Her novel also has Mordecai's prayer from Addition C *in nuce*. The parallels between the two are unmistakable (see the figure on p. 84). It is clear that Wolf crafted Mordecai's prayer utilizing Addition C (LXX).

Even more intriguing than explicit usage of these expansive traditions, most popular retellings share the same basic perspective on a number of points in the narrative. To illustrate this, I want to make note of three major commonalities between these ancient translations and our contemporary popular retellings of the Esther story. These commonalities include an emphasis on faith and piety in the story, the downplaying or justifying of Esther's presence in the pagan court, and the introduction of hostility towards Esther and/or the Jews more broadly prior to the competition of Esther 2:1–18.

37. Wolf, *Reluctant Queen*, 27–29.
38. Ibid., 50.

NRSV Esther 13:9–11, 15–17 (Addition C)	Mordecai's prayer in *A Reluctant Queen*[40]
He said, "O Lord, Lord, you rule as King over all things, for the universe is in your power and there is no one who can oppose you when it is your will to save Israel, for you have made heaven and earth, and every wonderful thing under heaven. You are Lord of all, and there is no one who can resist you, the Lord. [skipping vv.12–14 of the prayer] And now, O Lord God and King, God of Abraham, spare your people; for the eyes of our foes are upon us to annihilate us, and they desire to destroy the inheritance that has been yours from the beginning. Do not neglect your portion, which you redeemed for yourself out of the land of Egypt. Hear my prayer, and have mercy upon your inheritance; turn our mourning into feasting that we may live and sing praise to your name, O Lord; do not destroy the lips of those who praise you."	"O Lord God, almighty King, all things are in Your power. You made heaven and earth and every wonderful thing under the heavens. You are Lord of all, and there is no one who can resist You. Lord God, King, God of Abraham, spare Your people, for our enemies plan our ruin and are bent upon destroying the inheritance that You gave to us. Do not spurn us, whom You redeemed for yourself out of Egypt. Hear my prayer; have pity on Your people and turn our sorrow into joy; thus we shall live to sing praise to Your name, O Lord. Do not silence those who praise You."

Emphasis on Faith and Piety

Throughout the Greek and Aramaic translations we have seen a strong emphasis on the personal devotion of the Jewish characters. In the popular retellings of the story, Esther and Mordecai are also very devout and pious Jews. In the film *One Night with the King*, Esther has a special necklace that projects images of the Star of David upon the walls when light shines into it, which—never mind the blatant anachronism—is meant to demonstrate Esther's deep spiritual connection with the faith of her ancestors.[39] In *A Reluctant Queen*, Mordecai belongs to the stricter of two sects of Judaism within Susa, the one that "held strictly to the Mosaic Law."[40] Esther also

---

39. The film *Esther and the King* (1960) likewise depicts multiple Star of David images as part of the decor for the Jewish assembly.

40. Wolf, *Reluctant Queen*, 3.

prays at several points throughout the book to her "Father in Heaven," and even cites the famous "Shema" from Deuteronomy 6:4–5.[41] In Norah Lofts's novel *Esther*, Mordecai was placed in charge of genealogies in case any Jew feared that their pedigree might be lost "and his chance of fore-fathering the promised Messiah be obscured."[42]

When Mordecai is faced with the prospect of bowing before Haman we see this piety on full display in the popular versions. In *One Night with the King*, Mordecai declared boldly that he bows to his King alone—"The Great I Am, the one true God, the maker of heaven and earth, the God of Abram, of Isaac, and of Jacob." In *Animated Stories from the Bible: Esther* (1993), after Mordecai refuses to bow, Haman declares, "You are not in Israel, Mordecai. This is Persia; in Persia I am God."

This devotion extends as well into a passionate longing for Jerusalem, the land, and the temple throughout the popular retellings. In the Aramaic Targums we saw that Mordecai had to be exiled to Susa a second time after returning to Jerusalem (*Tg. S.* 2:6), and Esther was specifically told that she could have whatever she wanted in the king's kingdom except the rebuilding of the Jerusalem temple (*Tg. R.* 5:3). In each case the expansion was clearly a way to show that these Jewish characters were centrally concerned with the land, Jerusalem, and the temple (see also Addition C in the LXX). However, as we saw in chapter 1 (*Esther & the Compromise*) this notion was entirely lacking from the Hebrew version. In a similar manner, the popular versions include this enhancement on the text. In Lofts's *Esther*, Mordecai is shown bursting into tears and rending his clothes at the sight of the sacred vessels from the Jerusalem temple being used in the king's palace as kitchenware.[43] We also see Esther's deep longing for Jerusalem when Mordecai arrived to inform her of the king's new edict to gather all the virgins. She mistakenly assumed that perhaps his news would be that the king had finally permitted the Jews to return. The narrator informs us that she was "voicing the dearest, the foremost hope for every Jew in Persia."[44] Similarly, in *Esther: The Star and Sceptre*, Esther is first introduced playing the harp and singing Psalm 137:1, "By waters of Babylon there we sat down and wept, when we remembered Zion."[45] Within their first conversation in

41. Ibid., 72, 268.

42. Lofts, *Esther*, 41.

43. Ibid.

44. Ibid., 43.

45. Andrews, *Esther*, 32.

the narrative, Esther and Mordecai discuss Cyrus's role in Isaiah's prophecy to let the Jews return.[46] At a later point, Haman expressed his annoyance that the Jews send their wealth to Jerusalem.[47] We even see the Jews debate among themselves whether or not their bones should be buried in a foreign land, recalling Joseph's request to have his bones buried in the promised land rather than in Egypt (see Gen 50:25).[48] The same is also the case in the film *One Night with the King*, where Esther and Mordecai banter about Esther's desire to go to Jerusalem to "see our people restored" instead of remaining in the "pagan empire" after a caravan from Jerusalem arrived in Susa. In a later sequence she tells Mordecai how she longs to dance in Jerusalem like David danced.[49]

Esther's Presence in the Pagan Court Is Downplayed or Justified

In the ancient translations Esther loathes the bed of the king (Addition C in the LXX), and she is depicted as praying for thirty days in order to avoid going before the king (*Tg. S.* 4:11). Along these lines there are several ways in which the popular versions downplay or justify Esther's involvement with the pagan king. The first is simply the general attempt to de-sexualize the story. In *A Reluctant Queen*, the king complains about all the "interviews" that he has to conduct, saying, "These interviews are not only time consuming, they are extremely tedious."[50] In Lofts's novel *Esther*, the competition merely includes "an hour or so" conversation over a meal.[51] When it was Esther's turn to go before the king in Loft's novel, instead of having sex, she tells the king about the story of Samson from Judges,[52] and a similar thing takes place in the film *One Night with the King*, when Esther simply tells the king about the love story of Jacob and Rachel from Genesis. In *Veggie Tales* (2000) the competition is a rather innocuous talent show,

46. Ibid., 34–35.

47. Ibid., 69.

48. Ibid., 127.

49. This part about David dancing in Jerusalem is highly ironic. When David danced before the Lord (2 Sam 6:14–16) his wife Michal thought it was unbecoming for a king (2 Sam 6:20), but David rebuked her and she became infertile (2 Sam 6:21–23). And then comes the irony—this woman was a distant relative of Esther since Michal was a daughter of Saul.

50. Wolf, *Reluctant Queen*, 71.

51. Lofts, *Esther*, 37, 56.

52. Ibid., 70.

which Esther wins by singing a song about how she can face her fears with God on her side.

Most of the retellings also show Esther struggling with the prospect of going before the king in the competition and the idea of potentially marrying him. In *Esther: The Star and the Sceptre*, Esther requests to be alone before she goes to the king during the competition. The narrator informs us that Esther's handmaidens have become accustomed to her "religious ways" because "she spent more time praying than anyone else they knew."[53] As noted in chapter 1 (*Esther & the Compromise*), one of the issues naturally raised by mixed marriage was the purity of the religion of the Jews. This would therefore naturally affect the children who would grow up in a religiously divided household. In Heather Moore's novel *Esther: The Queen*, Esther struggles with this very thing and laments to God that her children "will be raised to worship Ahura-Mazda" and will "not be taught the law of Moses" or "observe the Sabbath."[54] As a solution to this in her narrative, Moore writes an epilogue that takes place on the one-year anniversary of Esther's marriage. Esther had made an agreement with her husband that "their children would be taught both religions, and they would be allowed to choose as they reached adulthood."[55] When Esther hears of the king's decree regarding the assembly of virgins in Lofts's *Esther*, she is immediately reluctant because of the "avoidance of mixed marriages" among her people.[56] As for Mordecai, we are told (anachronistically) that he was meant to betroth Esther to "some orthodox Jew."[57] When Mordecai tells Esther about the king's decree in *Esther: The Star and the Sceptre*, and explains what will be required of her sexually, the narrator informs us, "Raised in the Jewish tradition of the Law and the family as the basis for all of life, Hadassah found this shocking."[58] Indeed, during the competition to replace Vashti, Esther considers killing herself instead of going before the king, believing that God would be more pleased that way.[59]

In addition to downplaying pagan marriage, the popular versions also skirt the issue of eating pagan food in the pagan court. As we saw earlier in

53. Andrews, *Esther*, 113.

54. H. Moore, *Esther the Queen*, 154.

55. Ibid., 217.

56. Lofts, *Esther*, 45.

57. Ibid., 42.

58. Andrews, *Esther*, 77.

59. Ibid., 106.

this chapter, the ancient translations specifically added clarifications that Esther was not breaking any dietary laws (see Addition C in the LXX; *Tg. S.* 2:9; *Tg. R.* 3:8). *Tg. R.* even tried to clear the air about any possible involvement of Mordecai with the pagan feast from Esther 1 (*Tg. R.* 1:7), even though other Jews disobediently did (*Tg. R.* 4:1). This same perspective can be seen in the films and novels. In the film *One Night with the King*, Esther is shown in the king's palace throwing pieces of pork off of her plate for the monkeys to eat. In Moore's *Esther the Queen*, we read of Esther's initial experience in the king's palace: "One of the dishes held meat that looked like pork with an orange glaze, which Esther couldn't eat because of the law of Moses."[60] At Esther's wedding with the king, Moore writes that Esther "didn't have trouble partaking only what was allowed by the law of Moses" since there was a large selection of food available.[61] In addition to eating certain kinds of food, there was also the issue of how various food items were prepared. In *A Reluctant Queen*, we read of Jewish markets where meat was ritually killed and dressed by trained Jewish butchers.[62] Again in Moore's novel *Esther the Queen*, she writes regarding Esther's experience in the palace, "She didn't touch the meats, even though some of it was clean according to the law, but she assumed it had not been prepared according to the law. Outside her own community, few butchers followed the Mosaic practices."[63]

Introduction of Hostility before the Competition in Esther 2:1–18

There is one interesting trend among the ancient translations and the popular retellings. As far as I can tell, they all seem to provide a compelling hostility toward the Jews prior to Esther becoming queen in Esther 2:1–18. The introduction of Haman or general Jewish hostility prior to the competition is often provided as a rationale for the concealment of Esther's identity, which was for the purpose of winning the competition and gaining political leverage with the king in order to thwart the imminent threat.[64]

60. H. Moore, *Esther the Queen*, 61.

61. Ibid., 112.

62. Wolf, *Reluctant Queen*, 9.

63. H. Moore, *Esther the Queen*, 65.

64. We saw many commentators taking this perspective in chapter 2 (pp. 32–33), as well.

In the ancient translations this is clear from Addition A (LXX) where Mordecai's dream includes two fighting dragons. In the same Addition, Haman begins to resent Mordecai for his promotion and so decides to kill the Jews. The introduction of Haman as Memuchan in *Tg. R.* 1:16, and the reference to the possibility that the king may want to kill the Jews in *Tg. S.* 2:9–10, shows the consistency among the ancient translations in this regard. Surprisingly, this pattern can also be found throughout the contemporary popular versions too. For instance, in the *Veggie Tales* version, it is Haman who announces the king's edict regarding the gathering of the virgins. When he arrives on the scene Mordecai urgently declares, "It's Haman! That guy hates me!" In the cartoon *Animated Stories from the Bible: Esther*, the story begins prior to all the events recorded in the book of Esther with Mordecai receiving a young baby Esther into his custody. At this early stage in the narrative we are introduced to the conflict between Haman and Mordecai when Haman declared that he wished all Jews were slaves. Once the edict to assemble all the eligible virgins to the palace was decreed, Mordecai evaluated this edict in the light of the hostility toward the Jews and therefore commanded Esther to keep her ethnicity a secret in order to win the competition. Likewise, in Lofts's novel *Esther*, the opening scene takes place at a banquet in the royal palace prior to the banquet recorded in Esther 1. A young torchbearer looks upon the grandeur of the palace with tears in his eyes, seeing specifically the sacred vessels from the temple in Jerusalem. When the king asks him why he cries, he declares:

> My lord, I am an Amalekite. We are a small people, but for many years we fought the Jews and we had our successes. And our failures. I rejoice to see the symbols, the vessels of the false god of our enemies, put to their rightful purpose, the glorification of the King who has no equal upon this earth.[65]

This is Haman, of course. Later, Mordecai informs Esther that Haman is "a confirmed Jew-hater" as he tries to convince her to enter the competition to stop him.[66] The idea of strategic concealment is also found elsewhere in the films: *Esther and the King*; *The Book of Esther*; *One Night with the King*; *The Bible: Esther*; the cartoon *The Greatest Adventure: Stories from the Bible: Queen Esther*; as well as the novel *A Reluctant Queen*.

65. Lofts, *Esther*, 16–17.
66. Ibid., 48.

The general tenor of most films, cartoons, and novels on Esther follows the spirit of the expansive Greek and Aramaic texts instead of the Hebrew, as we have seen throughout this section. In most of these cases the producers/authors were no doubt trying to retell the *Hebrew version* and show no signs of direct influence from the Greek versions. By adding religious imagery and Jewish customs to the Hebrew version of Esther in any capacity—whether it is in a popular retelling, a commentary, a pastor's sermon, or a Sunday school lesson—the intuition and trajectory of the ancient translators are being followed. This makes the comment by Webb, that the rejection of the Greek additions by the Reformers "effectively blocked the way to any appropriation of Esther which involved moralizing,"[67] rather ironic. I will have more to say about why Protestants rejected the Greek expansions in the next chapter, but apparently the Reformers were not effective enough. We must therefore resist the temptation to follow the intuition of those who expanded the story in the past and those who are still doing it today.

Conclusion & Summary

The way that the Greek and Aramaic translations of Esther transformed the Hebrew story, not to mention the way contemporary versions have done this, completely changes the original intentions. Perhaps an illustration will aid us in thinking about the relationship between the translations and the Hebrew text. The additional material provided by the Greek and Aramaic versions should be thought of as unlike *The Lord of the Rings* and more like *The Wizard of Oz*. And here, for the illustration, I have in mind the films in particular. With the case of *The Lord of the Rings* there are several hours of additional material found on the DVDs. However, these additional scenes and sequences do not alter the theatrical versions or provide reinterpretations of events. The additions were written, produced, and performed by the same people.[68] In the case of *The Wizard of Oz*, however, the "additions" to the story function quite differently. In the original 1939 film, the Wicked Witch of the West was a bad witch who intended to cause chaos on all the Ozians. In this setting, Dorothy was surprised to meet the charming witch Glinda; "I've never heard of a beautiful witch before," she exclaimed. But Glinda explained to her, "Only bad witches are ugly." In a revision of

67. Webb, *Five Festal Garments*, 129.

68. I am not interested here in whether the additional scenes, or the theatrical versions, are faithful to J. R. R. Tolkien's original novels.

the story, Stephen Schwartz's musical *Wicked* depicts these two witches as former college roommates. Elphaba (the name given to the Wicked Witch) was not the malicious figure everyone had always thought. Rather, she was simply misunderstood because of circumstances beyond her control, such as being born with green skin. It is as if Glinda's words in *The Wizard of Oz* about ugliness and bad witches have been exposed for their inherent prejudices, being a veiled expression for "only uglies are bad." In a similar, though divergent manner, the prequel, *Oz the Great and Powerful* (2013), depicts Theodora (the name given to the Wicked Witch) as an originally well-intentioned woman. Her downfall was ultimately due to the fact that she was duped by her sister. For this reason Oz can say at the end of the film, "I know your wickedness is not your doing." Both *Wicked* and *Oz the Great and Powerful* are independent prequels that create their own backstories to *The Wizard of Oz*. Each prequel transforms the character of the Wicked Witch into something far different from the original intentions of the 1939 film. In the same manner, the character of Esther has been transformed in the Greek and Aramaic translations into something that she was never meant to be.[69]

In the light of the consistent way that the popular retellings share a similar perspective as the ancient translations, perhaps the version of Esther that many have inherited as a result has more in common with the Greek and Aramaic translations than the Hebrew story. It appears that many contemporary communicators of the Esther story have a similar intuition as the earliest translators, and have shaped contemporary readers to share the same intuition. This contemporary intuition follows the same trajectory as the ancient: the protagonists are made into religious and moral exemplars, the rough parts are smoothed over, and the parts that are meant to make readers blush are childproofed.

As a conclusion to part 1, this chapter, along with the previous two, has attempted to build the cumulative case that the Esther story presents secular and assimilated characters, who, although they experienced a profound deliverance, did not petition God's activity, or attribute their survival to his protection. This was seen in the case of the previous two chapters

---

69. The correspondence is greatest between how the prequel films function in relation to *The Wizard of Oz* and how Addition A functions for the Greek versions. Yet most of the second half of *Wicked* takes place simultaneously with the events depicted in *The Wizard of Oz* and in that regard functions similarly to Additions C and D of the Greek versions, as well as the rest of the religious expansions throughout both the Greek and Aramaic translations.

by looking closely at the Hebrew version of the story, and by seeing, in this chapter, how the secularity has bothered both ancient and modern interpreters enough that they felt the need to correct it, and to control the interpretation of others through the production of their religiously explicit editions.

So then, if the Hebrew story of Esther really is secular after all, how are we to make sense of it theologically? Is such a book worthy to belong in the canon of Scripture? If so, how does this message of the survival of God's unfaithful people fit within the canon? Can such a message fit? How does the church make sense of this for today? These questions will set the agenda for part 2.

Part Two

*Canonical & Theological
Reflections on a Secular Story*

4

Esther & the Canon

If someone asked you, perhaps over coffee, to summarize the Bible in one phrase or sentence, what would you say? Think about this for a moment. Certainly, it is a hard task. Once you have thought of a good summary sentence or phrase for the Bible as a whole try to apply it to *each of the books of the Bible individually*. Does it fit in each case? What did you pick? *God's story of salvation? The kingdom of God? God's covenant with humanity? God's presence?* Whatever you chose, how does it fit with the story of Esther? Does it work? In the light of our study up to this point, the problem with applying any overarching summary to Esther is twofold: (1) the protagonists do not seem to walk in step with what we might expect from Bible characters, and (2) there is a major omission from the story: *God himself*. Finding God in Esther is more difficult than any *Where's Waldo*™ puzzle, guaranteed.

Creating a single sentence or phrase to convey the message of each biblical book might seem reductionistic to most. But this exercise helps shed some light on the uncomfortable position that Esther holds within the Bible. Does Esther *really* belong in the canon? If so, how does it fit? Collectively, the present chapter and the following (part 2) seek to address these theological and canonical concerns in relation to the secular story analyzed in part 1.

For the purposes of the present chapter—determining whether Esther belongs in the canon in the first place—we will need to take a look (albeit a brief one) at what the canon is, how it came about, and how Esther was received and treated by both Christian and Jewish communities. So then, the starting point is determining what we mean by "canon." Biblical theologian

Brevard Childs offers this helpful definition of the canon that we will adopt for this study:

> The term canon points to the received, collected, and interpreted material of the church and thus establishes the theological context in which the tradition continues to function authoritatively for today.[1]

This is a helpful working definition of the canon for our purposes, and in utilizing it, we are provoked to ask, in what sense does Esther help to establish the "theological context" of the Christian tradition? What is Esther's contribution to theology if the Jewish characters appear as secular and assimilated as we saw in part 1?

We will begin to answer these questions in this chapter by looking at the reception of Esther. As we will see, Esther's reception history further corroborates the interpretation of part 1. Not only did some ancient interpreters change the story to make it fit "biblical tradition" (as we saw in chapter 3), we will see that some even rejected the book. Yet despite the strong negative response to Esther in some quarters, we will ultimately conclude this chapter by affirming that Esther does indeed belong in the canon after all. This will then set up the concluding theological reflection on Esther in the final chapter (*Esther & the Church*).

A Brief Overview of the Reception of Esther

Esther among Christians

The book of Esther has maintained an uncomfortable position within the Christian canon throughout the history of the church. Melito, who was the bishop of Sardis during the second century CE, made the earliest list recording the extent of the canonical books from the Old Testament, and his list did not include Esther.[2] In the fourth century CE, Amphilochius, the bishop of Iconium, stated that Esther was "accepted only by some."[3] Athanasius, the defender of orthodox Trinitarian theology at the council of Nicea in 325 CE, showed some uncertainty about Esther by placing it in a middle position between canonical and "apocryphal."[4] It is also suggestive

---

1. Childs, *Biblical Theology*, 71.
2. Law, *When God Spoke Greek*, 123; Schultz, "Book of Esther," 11.
3. Cited in Huey, "Esther," 783.
4. See Athanasius's *Epist. Test.*, as noted by Schultz, "Book of Esther," 11.

of the widespread opinion about Esther that only a single quotation from it can be found among all of the Antiochian church fathers, which came from the famous preacher John Chrysostom ("Golden Mouth").[5] In fact, a number of significant fourth-century bishops and theologians from the early church denied Esther's canonical status, including: Gregory of Nazianzus, Theodore of Mopsuestia, and more.[6] It was finally at the end of the fourth century that Esther was accepted as canonical at the Council of Hippo in 393 CE and the Council of Carthage in 397 CE.[7] However, the text that was accepted was the expanded Greek text, *not the Hebrew*. Despite being included in the canon at the end of the fourth century, the first commentary written by a Christian came centuries later when Rhabanus Maurus, Archbishop of Mainz, composed a commentary on Esther in the ninth century.[8] However, Maurus's commentary did not wrestle with the details of the text but rather read the story through an allegorical and christological lens.[9]

At the time of the Protestant Reformation, there was a reevaluation of the Greek translation of Esther (LXX). The Protestants deemed that solely the Hebrew text should function as authoritative whereas the Catholics accepted the Greek translation in the LXX as "deuterocanonical" (lit., "second canon") as well, along with the other "apocryphal" books (lit. "hidden") at the Council of Trent (1545–1563).[10] Even though Protestants accepted the Hebrew version as canonical, this does not mean that all equally held Esther in high esteem. In fact, we can see that Esther was poorly received among Protestants even at the very beginning. For instance, John Calvin did not write a single sermon or commentary on the book of Esther.[11] More explicitly, Martin Luther stated in his *Table Talk* (XXIV), "I am so great an enemy to the second book of the Maccabees, and to Esther, that I wish they had not come to us at all, for they have too many heathen unnaturalities."[12] Some later Protestant scholars even agreed with Luther on this. Otto

---

5. De Troyer, *Rewriting the Sacred Text*, 74.

6. See C. Moore, *Daniel, Esther, and Jeremiah*, 156.

7. B. Anderson, "Place of the Book of Esther," 33; Webb, *Five Festal Garments*, 129; Huey, "Esther," 783.

8. Bush, *Ruth, Esther*, 277.

9. See his comments in Conti and Pilara, "Esther," 397 (and elsewhere).

10. Moore, *Daniel, Esther, Jeremiah*, 156; Jobes and Silva, *Invitation to the Septuagint*, 81.

11. Jobes, *Esther*, 21.

12. Luther, *Table Talk*, 13.

Eissfeldt, an Old Testament scholar, would later concur, "For Christianity Luther's remark should be determinative."[13] L. B. Paton wrote that Luther's response was "not too severe."[14] Indeed, Paton went further, "The book is so conspicuously lacking in religion that it should never have been included in the Canon of the OT, but should have been left with Judith and Tobit among the 'apocryphal' writings."[15]

Esther among Jews

The controversy surrounding Esther was not unique to Christian interpreters. From 1947 to 1956, significant archeological discoveries were made from eleven caves west of the Dead Sea at Qumran in which manuscripts of every book of the Old Testament, except for the book of Esther, were recovered.[16] These manuscripts are commonly known as the Dead Sea Scrolls. The lack of manuscript evidence for Esther among these scrolls is remarkable considering three facts.

The first is the sheer abundance of manuscripts found at Qumran. Although it is well known that biblical manuscripts were found among the scrolls, these biblical manuscripts make up less than one-quarter of the roughly 930 manuscripts that were discovered.[17] Additional texts include previously known "apocryphal" and pseudepigraphical works, as well as unique sectarian documents, legal texts, hymnic materials, and calendars. Many of these new documents were likely written by the occupants of the settlement located near the caves, and these occupants were most likely the Essenes.[18]

Second, archeological evidence suggests that occupation of the Qumran site began sometime between 100 to 50 BCE[19] and ended with

13. See Eissfeldt, *Introduction*, 511–12, cited in Bush, *Ruth, Esther*, 332.

14. Paton, *Critical and Exegetical Commentary*, 96.

15. Ibid., 97.

16. See Vanderkam, *Dead Sea Scrolls Today*, 49–50.

17. Ibid., 49.

18. According to Josephus, the Essenes were one of the major "philosophies" of Judaism (Josephus, *Life*, 10). Pliny the Elder stated that the Essenes were located "on the west side of the Dead Sea" and that Engedi was lying "below" (*infra hos*). See Pliny, *Natural History* 5.73. This description of their location, although anachronistic due to its destruction at the time that Pliny wrote this, is nevertheless remarkably compatible with the actual location of the site. See Milik, *Ten Years of Discovery in the Wilderness of Judaea*, 45.

19. Magness, *Archaeology of Qumran*, 63–64.

the Jewish War in 70 CE.[20] Esther was therefore an available text for a few centuries prior to this period and so probably would have been known by the community members at Qumran. Additionally, regardless of when Esther was written,[21] both the tale about Esther and the origin of Purim predate the composition and are presupposed by it (Esth 9:16–32). Thus it is hardly likely that the occupants of Qumran would have been unfamiliar with Esther.

Third, copies of Esther would have been multiplied in order to ensure that it was read during the annual celebration of Purim.[22] So when an often-copied text shows up missing among a large repository of texts, we should consider whether its absence is a sign of rejection.[23]

There are at least two theological reasons why Esther was likely rejected by the Qumran community,[24] which point toward the conclusion that its absence from the Dead Sea Scrolls collection was not an accident of history. The first reason is because the community at Qumran adhered to the Mosaic law strictly and even developed their own unique sectarian regulations, as seen in their various "Rules" (e.g., 1QM, 1QS, 4QMMT, 11QT). Such a strict community would not have approved of the overall secularity of the Jewish characters in the story (as argued in part 1 of this study). The second theological reason is that the Qumran community would never have embraced Purim as a sacred festival. The authoritative festivals were the ones found in the Torah, and Purim has no claim to such authority. Furthermore, Purim would not have fit within the unique calendar system at Qumran, which was a solar calendar rather than the lunar calendar of

---

20. De Vaux, *Archeology and the Dead Sea Scrolls*, 36; Magness, *Archaeology of Qumran*, 61.

21. I think it most likely that Esther was written in the fifth or fourth century BCE near the end of the Persian Empire or the very beginning of the Hellenistic period (as suggested by Jobes, *Esther*, 28–30). Yet Fox (*Character and Ideology*, 139–40) gives Esther a Hellenistic setting.

22. Beckwith, "Formation of the Hebrew Bible," 76.

23. Some have contended that although there are no extant manuscripts of the Esther story, there are actually allusions to the story in 4Q550 and the *Temple Scroll* (11QT) 64:9 (see Vermes, *Complete Dead Sea Scrolls*, 11). However, these "allusions" are too general to allude to the Esther story proper, and thus it is best to conclude that these are fragments from similar kinds of narratives of court intrigue from the Persian period (see Berlin, *Esther*, xliv). De Troyer concludes similarly on 4Q550 yet states that the *Temple Scroll* (11QT) is reminiscent of Esther. See De Troyer, *End of the Alpha Text*, 36; idem, "Once More," 401–21.

24. So VanderKam and Flint, *Meaning of the Dead Sea Scrolls*, 119.

mainstream Judaism. The solar calendar was organized in such a way that no festival would fall on the Sabbath (except for the festivals prescribed for a full seven days), because the community at Qumran was very strict regarding Sabbath observance. The day for celebrating Purim, the fourteenth of Adar, would always fall on the Sabbath in their system, which would have created problems for the community's observance of the festival.[25] Thus, for these reasons it seems likely that the Qumran community rejected the book of Esther as well as Purim.

It is likely that for sensibilities such as those at Qumran the Hebrew text was altered so significantly in the Greek and Aramaic translations (as seen in chapter 3: *Esther & the Cover-Up*). Similar sensibilities as the Qumran community could also be seen in the fact that various rabbis denied the divine inspiration of Esther, debating whether or not the book "defiled the hands," which specifically referred to its authoritative status.[26]

Later Jewish evidence demonstrates, however, that it eventually became a well-loved and cherished book by the Jews. There are in fact more manuscripts for Esther than any other book from the Old Testament besides the Torah.[27] This is largely due to the strong embrace of the book among Jews, rather than Christians. Rabbi Simeon ben Lakish (ca. 300 CE) asserted, "When Messiah comes, the other books of the Old Testament may pass away, but the Torah and Esther will abide forever."[28] This appreciation was obviously not quite the same among Christians. Yet it remained enormously popular among Jews and Jewish exegetes, perhaps due to the very fact that the Christians did not appreciate it.[29]

Does Esther Belong in the Canon?

With this brief overview of the reception of Esther we have seen how various Christians and Jews responded to the story. The Christian response tended not to be too positive, and although the Jewish response started off quite ambiguous it eventually became a much-loved story. This history further corroborates the interpretation offered in part 1 since so many people had difficulty reconciling whether Esther should be given any sort

25. Beckwith, "Formation of the Hebrew Bible," 77; Berlin, *Esther*, xlv.

26. Beckwith, "Formation of the Hebrew Bible," 59–64.

27. Breneman, *Ezra, Nehemiah, Esther*, 292.

28. Cited in Huey, "Irony as the Key," 36.

29. Walfish, *Esther in Medieval Garb*, 75.

of authoritative, canonical, or scriptural status. So then, does the Hebrew version of Esther, with all of its secularity, belong in the canon?

There are, of course, various kinds of canons that function authoritatively for their respective traditions. For Jews, the canon consists of the *Tanakh*: the Torah, the Prophets, and the Writings (sometimes called "The Hebrew Bible"). These books correspond to the same thirty-nine books of the Protestant Old Testament, though the books are listed in a different order. In ancient times some groups within broader Judaism, such as the Samaritans and the Sadducees, regarded only the five books of the Torah as authoritative, and the Samaritans even had their own unique version of it. Marcion, the gnostic heretic from the early church, regarded only ten of the thirteen Pauline Epistles and the Gospel of Luke to be canonical (all of which were significantly modified), disregarding the rest of the New Testament and all of the Old Testament.[30] Catholics and the Orthodox traditions include all the same books in the Old Testament and New Testament as the Protestants but also include the "apocryphal" writings. For some strands within Orthodoxy, such as the Ethiopian Orthodox Church, even more texts are also included as Scripture, like *Jubilees* and *1 Enoch*.[31] Mormons and Jehovah's Witnesses, groups which are outside of traditional Christianity, regard the same sixty-six books of the Protestant canon to be authoritative, though they each regard only a single translation of that canonical material to be authoritative: the *King James Version* for Mormons and the *New World Translation of the Holy Scriptures* for the Jehovah's Witnesses. In distinction to the Jehovah's Witnesses, Mormons include additional materials within their canon: *The Book of Mormon*, *The Doctrine and Covenants*, and *The Pearl of Great Price*. The Mormon canon is also an "open canon," meaning that additional Scriptures could be added with new revelation. For this study, the canon that I am particularly interested in is the Protestant canon; the Christian canon that claims that the Hebrew version of Esther is to be regarded as exclusively authoritative, unlike the Orthodox and

---

30. Longenecker, *Galatians*, xliii. Contemporary "hyper-dispensationalists" follow a related pattern. Those who espouse this radical form of dispensationalism create a sharp dichotomy between Israel and the church in their theological framework and thus regard only the Pauline epistles written to the Gentiles as authoritative for the contemporary Gentile church (and there is debate among themselves whether portions of Acts are relevant as well). However, unlike Marcion they do not denigrate the God of the Old Testament. They simply "divide" the word of truth (1 Tim 2:15; KJV) according to the appropriate dispensation in God's economy.

31. Law, *When God Spoke Greek*, 59.

the Catholics who accept the expansive Greek translation (though for the Catholics this acceptance is through its transmission in the Latin Vulgate).

So then, for those who embrace the Hebrew version of Esther we need to ask whether it belongs in the canon. Some however may not find this question worthwhile. Samuel Wells, for instance, stated that the question of Esther's canonicity is one in which there is no value addressing. The reason, Wells states, is because "it has been there for most of two millenniums, and Christian theology has taken shape assuming its presence there."[32] Surely the book of Esther has been part of the received canonical literature of the Christian church for many centuries, but it is entirely misleading to state that "Christian theology has taken shape" under the assumption of its canonicity. Rather it seems like Christian theology has largely ignored Esther and has been fairly indifferent to its theological contribution. If it is the case, as Karen Jobes has said, that Esther is "perhaps the most striking biblical statement of what systematic theologians call *the providence of God*,"[33] then why do theologians largely neglect the book of Esther in their formulation of doctrines, including providence? For example, Esther is not cited at all in W. Shedd's *Dogmatic Theology* or Karl Barth's *Church Dogmatics* or W. Pannenberg's three-volume *Systematic Theology*, and Esther is cited only once in Louis Berkhof's *Systematic Theology*[34] and John Calvin's *Institutes of the Christian Religion*.[35] Most ironically of all, a biblical-theological book by Walt Kaiser, entitled *Recovering the Unity of the Bible: One Continuous Story, Plan, and Purpose*, fails to mention Esther. This makes one wonder if Esther has anything to contribute to the Bible after all.

But, since Esther is found in the Bible, surely it must have passed various criteria for determining the extent of canonical literature, right? For the New Testament collection, many point to apostolic authority (authorship or oversight) as a determinative criterion. In regards to the inclusion of the Old Testament and the exclusion of the Apocrypha, Protestants point to the fact that the "apocryphal" texts were not accepted by mainstream Judaism. Some offer another criterion for separating the Apocrypha from the Old Testament as canonical Scriptures—citations in the New Testament. As an example of this, Wayne Grudem makes the use of the Old Testament in the

---

32. Wells and Sumner, *Esther & Daniel*, 10.

33. Jobes, *Esther*, 43 (emphasis original).

34. Berkhof, *Systematic Theology*, 427.

35. Calvin, *Institutes*, 820.

New Testament a major factor for including the Old Testament collection of books within the canon. He states:

> According to one count, Jesus and the New Testament authors quote various parts of the Old Testament Scriptures as divinely authoritative over 295 times, but not once do they cite any statement from the books of the Apocrypha or any other writings as having divine authority. The absence of any such reference to other literature as divinely authoritative, and the extremely frequent reference to hundreds of places in the Old Testament as divinely authoritative, gives strong confirmation to the fact that the New Testament authors agreed that the established Old Testament canon, no more and no less, was to be taken as God's very words.[36]

Yet using this criterion to determine the extent of the Old Testament is problematic. If this principle is a useful guide for determining which books should be included in the canon, it certainly does not offer any guidance on which books should be excluded. This can be seen from three reasons. First, what are we to make of the many sources *cited in the Old Testament* that we have no access to? See the list below:[37]

- The book of the wars of the LORD (Num 21:14)

- The book of Jashar (Josh 10:13; 2 Sam 1:18)

- The book of the annals of Solomon (1 Kgs 11:41)

- The book of the annals of the kings of Israel (1 Kgs 14:19; 15:31; 16:5, 14, 20, 27; 22:39; 2 Kgs 1:18; 10:34; 13:8, 12; 14:15, 28; 15:11, 21, 26, 31; 2 Chr 20:34)

- The book of the annals of the kings of Judah (1 Kgs 14:29; 15:23; 22:45; 2 Kgs 8:23; 12:19; 14:18; 15:6, 36; 16:19; 20:20; 21:17, 25; 23:28; 24:5)

- The book of the annals of King David (1 Chr 27:24)

- The records of Samuel the seer (1 Chr 29:29)

- The records to Nathan the prophet (1 Chr 29:29; 2 Chr 9:29)

- The records of Gad the seer (1 Chr 29:29)

- The prophecy of Ahijah the Shilonite (2 Chr 9:29)

---

36. Grudem, *Systematic Theology*, 57.

37. The wording for each is taken from the NIV. It is difficult to discern whether some of these may be canonical books known by a different name and also whether some of them are even duplicates of each other.

- The visions of Iddo the seer (2 Chr 9:29; 10:15; 12:15; 13:22)

- The records of Shemaiah the prophet (2 Chr 12:15)

- The book of the kings of Judah and Israel (2 Chr 16:11; 25:26; 27:7; 28:26; 32:32; 33:18; 35:27; 36:8)

- The annals of Jehu son of Hanani (2 Chr 20:34)

- The annotations on the book of the kings (2 Chr 24:27)

- The records of the seers (2 Chr 33:19)

- The book of Truth (Dan 10:21)

These books are not included in the Protestant canon, or any other canon; there are simply no other records of these books. Might this imply that these books are missing from the Bible? Second, there are references to "non-canonical" texts in the New Testament, even though these are not from the literary corpus called the Apocrypha, such as the citations of *The Assumption of Moses* in Jude 9 and *1 Enoch* in Jude 14–15. In fact, allusions to other Jewish texts and traditions from both the Apocrypha and the Pseudepigrapha can be found throughout the New Testament.[38] How can we determine, using Grudem's criterion, that these citations were not considered "divinely authoritative"? Third, and most importantly, Esther is never cited directly nor is it alluded to in the New Testament.[39] This means that there is no explicit sanction from the New Testament authors that Esther was "divinely authoritative." So if Esther fails this criterion should we disregard the book? From these reasons we can see that this criterion simply fails to account for the extent of the Old Testament collection of books within the canon. Grudem's criterion may not be intended to be sufficient for determining the extent of the Old Testament, but given the points outlined above, is it actually helpful? If it continues to be upheld as a determining factor, we might be tempted to leave Esther behind.

Grudem concludes, however, despite listing other criteria, that the ultimate criterion of canonicity is divine authorship.[40] Surely this is something that can be affirmed from a position of faith, believing as well that the Holy Spirit guided the church in recognizing the proper documents

---

38. E.g., the allusions to traditions found in the Book of the Watchers (*1 Enoch* 6–36) in 1 Pet 3:18–22; 2 Pet 2:4; Jude 6.

39. Despite the attempt of Blomberg to see an echo of Esther 2:9 in Matthew 14:6. See Blomberg, "Matthew," 50.

40. Grudem, *Systematic Theology*, 67–68.

to be authoritative, but again, this would be impossible to prove. A more objective criterion, and no doubt the most basic and intuitive, is reception itself. For Protestants, it is particularly crucial to consider, in the case of the Old Testament, what books were received as canonical by Christians *and Jews* (hence the Protestant rejection of the so-called "apocryphal" books).

The criterion of reception helps us make sense of the issue of "missing" books. For instance, all those books cited earlier from the Old Testament (such as the book of Jashar, etc.) are not actually "missing" at all (from a canonical perspective). Surely those books, if found, would be of immense value for historical, cultural, and linguistic purposes, but they were not received as authoritative for doctrine or instructive for living. This is also helpful for thinking about the possibility that the Apostle Paul, for example, may have written other letters to other churches than the ones we have in our Bibles. In fact, Paul's letters themselves imply as much. In Paul's correspondence with the church at Corinth he refers to other letters that he wrote to them (1 Cor 5:9; 2 Cor 2:3–4; 7:8).[41] Likewise, Colossians 4:16 refers to a letter intended for the church in Laodicea. Some have suggested that this is actually a reference to the letter to the Ephesians since "in Ephesus" from Ephesians 1:1 is lacking from some important manuscripts,[42] and so theoretically could have been originally intended for Laodicea. The evidence regarding Marcion suggests that he assumed Ephesians was in fact written to the Laodiceans.[43] If these are not the same letter, however, then we have another clear example of a missing letter from Paul.[44] It is also not out of the realm of possibility that Paul wrote to other churches that had positive responses to his message, such as the Bereans mentioned in Acts 17:10–15. So we can conclude that the Apostle Paul wrote other letters that we do not have access to. And who knows about the other apostles? Regardless of what the answer is, from the perspective of reception there are no texts that are truly "missing" or "lost" in regards to the canon.

---

41. Due to the eclectic feel of 2 Corinthians it may be the case that it is an amalgam of these other correspondences, but such conjecture, although possible on internal grounds, does not find any evidence in the textual transmission.

42. Such as $\mathfrak{P}^{46}$, B, and ℵ.

43. Tertullian, *Adv. Marc.* V. 11 and 17.

44. The creation of a *Letter to the Laodiceans* found in the New Testament Apocrypha indicates that there was some fascination in knowing what Paul wrote to that church, implying that Ephesians was not universally considered to be the letter mentioned in Colossians 4:16.

The fact that there may be some apostolic writings that the church does not possess also raises the question of whether apostolicity is really a helpful criterion for determining the New Testament collection of books within the canon. Yet when we regard reception as the key criterion this completely fades away. The idea that Paul wrote other letters is interesting, but it plays no role in what the canon is. Even if archeologists were somehow able to uncover a hitherto undiscovered Pauline letter I would submit that such a text fails the ultimate criterion of canonicity—it was not *received* as canonical by the church. This is partly why Hal Taussig's *A New New Testament: A Bible for the 21st Century Combining Traditional and Newly Discovered Texts* is unwarranted from the very start. Not only are the added texts much later than the rest of the New Testament documents and filled with gnostic theology that is quite foreign to the early Christianity of the first century, but these texts were not received to be canonical by the church. Therefore, there can never be additions to the list of canonical texts.

So if we cannot add to the texts of the Bible, can we take some away, such as Esther? We may wonder if such a decision might be necessary for Esther, but we should consider a different example first as an illustration. What if Paul did not write all the epistles attributed to him? Some scholars suggest that this is the case. A distinction is made in scholarship between the seven "undisputed Pauline letters" (Romans, 1–2 Corinthians, Galatians, Philippians, 1 Thessalonians, and Philemon) and the six "disputed Pauline letters" (Colossians, Ephesians, 2 Thessalonians, 1–2 Timothy, and Titus). Without getting into every detail of this debate, I mention this issue for illustrative purposes. Personally, I regard all of the thirteen epistles attributed to Paul to be authentically Pauline. Yet it is important to realize that even this issue is not a *canonical* issue (as odd as that may sound). Once again, the ultimate criterion is reception, and these texts were received as authoritative and canonical. So even if, as some suggest, the "disputed Pauline Epistles" were written by disciples of Paul sometime after his death, this would not warrant dismissal from the canon. Indeed, these texts were received as canonical and we ought to trust the Spirit's guidance in the process. As Hays and Ansberry conclude, "The work of the Holy Spirit in the composition and canonization of the text serves as the locus of authority, not the putative author(s)."[45]

---

45. Hays and Ansberry, *Evangelical Faith*, 131.

Therefore, the received texts are the canonical texts. We cannot add books to the canon or omit them. Yet we must reckon with the fact that the version of Esther that was originally accepted by Christians as canonical was the religiously expansive Greek version. What do we do about that? The first thing that is important to remember is that the Hebrew version of Esther is the version that was received in the Jewish canon (the *Tanakh*), which Protestants take as a fact of no little significance. The second point is that although certain texts may have been received in certain forms, that does not preclude the role of textual criticism for determining the presence of interpolations. Thus, Protestants simply take Jerome's decision to place the six Additions from the Greek version of Esther at the end of his Latin translation one step further. And this text-critical issue is not unique to Esther. For instance, many would regard the so-called "Longer Ending of Mark" (Mark 16:9–20) and the *pericope adulterae* (John 7:53—8:11) to be secondary additions. In the same way, Protestants recognize that Esther was received as canonical and so include it, but it is the Hebrew text of Esther, without the Greek expansions, that is the canonical text.[46]

We saw in chapter 3 (*Esther & the Cover-Up*) how much more religious the Greek translations are over against what we have seen from the Hebrew story, and so it may seem counterintuitive to some readers that I am suggesting that Christians should embrace the "secular" text (the Hebrew MT) over a "religious" one (LXX or AT). Should we not just follow the trajectory and "go with the flow"? One representative voice advocating such a position is theologian David Brown. For him, revelation is part of a dialogue between the human and the divine. If at any point humans appropriate bits of the divine communication as "permanent" that God had only intended to be "provisional," Brown asks, "what could be more natural than that he should inspire a re-interpretation of the material in question such that it then gains a more appropriate and lasting significance?"[47] Thus, Brown views the Greek versions of Esther as a "divine corrective" that have "incomparably improved" the original "jingoistic and unreligious book."[48]

---

46. My arguments about the Greek traditions of Esther are in no way meant to undermine Timothy Michael Law's, *When God Spoke Greek*, which successfully demonstrates the centrality of the LXX in the development of early Christianity. With that said, my interest in the present study is strictly with Esther, which I take to have been an originally secular tale that the LXX intentionally sought to correct. Thus, my concern is to recover the suppressed Esther story.

47. Brown, *Divine Trinity*, 87–88.

48. Ibid., 89.

Brown concludes, "It is perhaps not too fanciful to suppose that [God] inspired someone to make suitable correctives to what was not incapable of being displaced from its special status as part of the process of divine dialogue."[49] Besides the fact that I do not think that God inspires Scripture like college students write term papers—as if the Hebrew version of Esther was God's "rough draft" that he followed up with the Greek—I regard such notions of "improvement" to miss the *God-intentioned* secularity of the Esther story.

Conclusion & Summary

So then, we can conclude that the book of Esther does indeed belong in the canon. It is not going anywhere. The conclusion of Jobes is worth citing here in full:

> In spite of the problems the book raises, the evangelical doctrine of Scripture does not permit us to dismiss any book of the canon as unworthy of our reverent attention. And Esther is undeniably a part of the canon for both synagogue and church. Although God himself is not mentioned in the story, because the book is in the Bible, in a sense God is telling us the story. He has inspired the biblical writer to narrate the events for subsequent generations. As the apostle Paul writes in Romans 15:4, "For everything that was written in the past was written to teach us, so that through endurance and encouragement of the Scriptures we might have hope." Thus, we can pick up the book of Esther with assurance that, despite first appearances, God has here given us bread and not a stone.[50]

I am sympathetic to Jobes's claim here that Scripture places a certain hermeneutical restraint upon believers. Yet, what we have discovered in this study is that a book's inclusion in the Bible does not mean that it is therefore meant to be interpreted a certain way, or that it automatically has a certain character or quality to it. Too often these sorts of assumptions distort the interpretation of Esther with a theological or canonical glaze. Just because the story of Esther is in the Bible does not mean that it cannot also be scandalous and secular. Indeed, I believe it is so.

49. Ibid., 90.
50. Jobes, *Esther*, 21–22.

But how then does Esther fit within the canon, within redemptive history, and within the basic storyline of the Bible? What is its theological contribution? Are the words of Hebrews 4:12 that God's word is "sharper than any two-edged sword" applicable to Esther? (Looking at the 75,810-person body count at the end of Esther there is at least one way that we can answer "yes" to this question). Should we just ignore Esther like many of the theologians throughout church history and ostensibly even the New Testament itself?

It may be that this lack of attention to Esther in the New Testament has afforded us with a unique opportunity to read the story for what it intends to be. As Brevard Childs explains:

> The significance of emphasizing the continuing canonical integrity of the Old Testament lies in resisting the Christian temptation to identify Biblical Theology with the New Testament's interpretation of the Old, as if the Old Testament's witness were limited to how it was once heard and appropriated by the early church. One of the major objections to the Tübingen form of Biblical Theology (Gese, Stuhlmacher) is that the Old Testament has become a horizontal stream of tradition from the past whose witness has been limited to its effect on subsequent writers. The Old Testament has thus lost its vertical, existential dimension, which as scripture of the church continues to bear its own witness within the context of the Christian Bible.[51]

What we should take from this point by Childs is that every verse of the Old Testament, and not simply those portions that have been cited in the New Testament, are part of Christian Scripture. We should not think that this implies that the New Testament authors misrepresented the Old Testament; but rather, we should be critical of the reductionistic perspective that is so prevalent within the church. This perspective fails to recognize the significance of entire Old Testament books—and not just simply the four or five citations of a particular book in the New Testament—as relevant and authoritative for Christians today. Since the New Testament does not quote or allude to the book of Esther, there is no "temptation," as Childs remarks, to reduce the theology of the book of Esther to how the New Testament authors understood and utilized the story. Thus, we are truly able to take our evaluation of the text from part 1 and see how Esther's unique voice

---

51. Childs, *Biblical Theology*, 77.

adds to the biblical choir. And when we glance across the canon in the final chapter we will see that Esther's song is quite beautiful.

5

Esther & the Church

If a Christian minister is faithful to the context, he will not take his text from
Esther; and, if the leader of a church-school class shows any Christian
discernment, he will not waste time trying to show that the heroes
of the book are models of character, integrity, and piety.[1]

—BERNHARD W. ANDERSON, 1950

Our study of the text of Esther in part 1 has shown that much of the
sentiment behind Anderson's quote above is accurate. The heroes are
not the pious exemplars that many have taken them to be. They were dis-
loyal to their covenant God and had forgotten his promises. Yet is Anderson
correct in suggesting that only when someone is *unfaithful* to Esther and
distorts its meaning that Esther would then be appropriate for sermons and
Sunday school? In other words, is it not possible that *a secular story could
function as Scripture for the Christian church*? What we have seen from the
present study is that the book of Esther is much more troublesome than
most of us would like. But does this mean that we ought to affirm with Anderson that Esther needs to be avoided on Sundays? Having concluded in
the previous chapter that Esther does indeed belong in the canon, despite
its glaring secularity and depiction of assimilation, we are now finally ready
to address how Esther *fits* in the canon and how it contributes theologically
to the message of the Bible. The answer that we will discover is this: *Esther*

1. B. Anderson, "Place of the Book of Esther," 42.

is a story of God's faithfulness to his unfaithful people. But this immediately begs the question, *where was Esther's elusive God anyway?*

The Elusive God of Esther

Here we return to the question that started this study: what do we make of the absence of religious imagery, Jewish custom, theology, and most importantly, God himself? As Anthony Tomasino asserts, "To say that this absence is unusual would be an understatement: Almost all ancient Near Eastern literature is permeated with religious language. The lack of religious references in the book of Esther is highly remarkable—and almost certainly intentional."[2] The question for us now is, *what exactly was the author's intent behind all of this?*

Absence as Reverence?

Some find that the omission of God is rooted in the nature of Esther as depicting the origins of a festival. Since Esther is to be read every year during the Festival of Purim, known for its frivolity, L. B. Paton concludes, "On such occasions the name of God might be profaned, if it occurred in the reading; and, therefore, it was deemed best to omit it altogether."[3] However, this might explain the absence of the divine name specifically (YHWH) and perhaps even some other divine titles and names (e.g., Adonai, El-Shaddai, Elohim, etc), but it hardly explains the lack of general religious imagery, Jewish customs, and theological beliefs.

Take the Greek text of 1 Maccabees as an example. The book of 1 Maccabees—which explains the origin of the Jewish festival Hanukkah just as Esther provides the origins for Purim—lacks the typical divine names and titles given to God in the Septuagint (e.g., *kyrios, theos*, etc). However, the similarity between Esther and 1 Maccabees goes no further.

2. Tomasino, "Esther," 472. Although he contends elsewhere in his commentary that "from another place" in Esther 4:14 is "an expression of faith in God, who will not allow his people to perish" and regards the fast of 4:16 as "designed to implore God's favor" (Tomasino, "Esther," 492), I certainly agree that the absence of God and religious imagery, let alone distinctly Jewish imagery, was intentional.

3. Paton, *Critical and Exegetical Commentary*, 95. So also C. Moore, *Daniel, Esther, and Jeremiah*, 157. Adele Berlin similarly notes that the absence of any reference to God is due to its genre, which she calls "a comedy for a carnivalesque festival" (Berlin, *Esther*, xli).

In 1 Maccabees, some Jews at that time (mid-second century BCE) were completely assimilating to the prevailing Hellenistic culture; Greek gymnasiums were being built for education in Greek philosophy and culture (1:14), the marks of circumcision were removed by some (1:15), and the covenant was abandoned (1:15). Antiochus IV Epiphanes, the Seleucid ruler, took the sacred utensils from the temple (1:22–23), sacrificed to idols and profaned the Sabbath (1:43), outlawed sacrifices made to Israel's God (1:45), sacrificed swine and other unclean animals in the temple (1:47), and prohibited circumcision (1:48). In defiance of these laws, a group of Jews determined not to eat unclean food (1:62), deciding that they preferred death over defilement (1:63). They were not going to let the religion and covenant of their ancestors be forsaken (2:19–20). Their defiance led to a revolution against the pagan empire which began when one pious Jew named Mattathias killed a fellow Jew who was making a pagan sacrifice (2:23–24). This revolution brought about a brief era of independence (the Hasmonean Dynasty) before the Jewish people were subsumed under Roman rule in 63 BCE.

Although 1 Maccabees lacks the typical divine names and titles for God, he is obliquely mentioned throughout the story as "Heaven" (1 Macc 3:16–17, 50; 4:10–11, 24, 40, 55; 5:31; 9:46; 12:15; see also "Heaven's mercy" in 16:3), and once as the "Savior of Israel" (4:30). Pronouns that refer to God were used as well. However, God is never called "God" or "Lord" in this book once. Additionally, there are various examples of religious imagery and Jewish customs. The Jews pray consistently, show concern for following the law of Moses, speak of the temple, sing praises and hymns to God, and even await a prophet for further direction (4:46), showing concern for God's direction. The piety and devotion is so strong in 1 Maccabees that the reason why God is not named is immediately intelligible; we can actually see this as an instance of piety and reverence. Yet such is manifestly not the case with Esther. Intriguingly, Hanukkah reflects God's deliverance of his faithful people, whereas Purim reflects the deliverance of an unfaithful people. Thus, the argument that Esther avoids reference to God out of reverence is unconvincing, especially since this explanation cannot also account for the lack of religious customs more broadly.

Human Ingenuity in the Face of Uncertainty?

Another possible explanation for the absence of God in Esther is that this points to the need for human ingenuity.[4] Indeed some take this line of thinking further and point to the uncertainty that provokes this need for human ingenuity. As an example of this, Fox suggests that the lack of reference to God is "an attempt to convey uncertainty about God's role in history."[5] Wells goes further, stating, "Esther is a meditation on what it means to be a Jew, opposed by the world and apparently abandoned by God, and yet with fathomless ingenuity and indomitable spirit."[6] For him, "Esther is a story of how a people profoundly hurt by the absence of their hitherto faithful God may end up believing in themselves."[7] Wells even finds a critique of God's reliability in the figure of the king:

> That Ahasuerus is a parody of God is a playful yet acerbic indication that God's ways seem arbitrary, God's faithfulness seems unreliable, and God's judgments seem fragile. The Feast of Passover is rivaled by the Feast of Purim, a celebration of luck, and chance, and coincidence, and of human endeavor, humor, irony, and wit. These are the new resources of the people of God.[8]

Yet it is not clear how the absence of God from the narrative points the reader toward questioning God's involvement when the characters themselves make no such connections. Uncertainty is not the same as indifference. If the interpretation of Fox and Wells was correct the characters would surely have expressed doubt or skepticism at some point in the narrative. The characters are not "uncertain" about God's activity; they are oblivious.

Providence or Coincidence, or Both?

Perhaps the most prominent interpretation is that the lack of explicit and direct reference to God is a witness to God's providential care. Some suggest

---

4. So Berg, *Book of Esther*, 111. Talmon regards the story of Esther as a "Wisdom" narrative. Thus, he suggests that the absence of God is part of its genre, pointing to the need for human wisdom in difficult situations (see Talmon, "'Wisdom' in the Book of Esther," 419–55).

5. Fox, *Character and Ideology*, 247.

6. Wells and Sumner, *Esther & Daniel*, 11.

7. Ibid.

8. Ibid., 58. See also Beckett, *Gospel in Esther*, 6–7.

that God's absence is actually an "invitation" to search for the hidden God in the text. For instance, Debra Reid suggests, "It could be maintained that the author is concerned with leading readers to their own faith-reading of the text, rather than imposing such a reading."[9] She adds, "Here I believe we move closer to the author's intentions."[10] David Clines regards the omissions of God to demonstrate that the author is "an Old Believer whose ultimate act of faith is to take the protective providence of God for granted."[11] Yet Clines believes that this same author systematically excised all religious imagery from an original version of the story, which does not sound like the activity of one who takes God's providence "for granted" (for more on this issue see the appendix).[12] Furthermore, Clines concludes that one of the primary theological elements of the story is that "the providence of God is to be relied on to reverse the ill-fortunes of Israel."[13] But how can this be the theology of the story when the characters themselves do not *rely* on God's providence at all? Do we ever read about Esther acknowledging that she reached her royal position as the result of God's providence and control? We do not. But we do read in Genesis about a similar pagan court tale in which Joseph told his brothers—the very people who betrayed him and sold him into slavery—that it was God who sent him to Egypt (Gen 45:5, 7–9), concluding ultimately that "you intended to harm me, but God intended it for good" (Gen 50:20a). Esther and Mordecai do not convey the assurance in God's providence that Joseph does. This is especially intriguing as a contrast in the light of the allusions to the Joseph narrative in the story of Esther.[14]

9. Reid, *Esther*, 49.

10. Ibid.

11. Clines, *Esther Scroll*, 156.

12. See ibid., 107–12, 151–58.

13. Ibid., 154.

14. The allusion to the Joseph story may imply that the author was intending for his audience to think about the story of Esther in relation to the story of Joseph. Yet what is intriguing about these similarities are the major differences between the contexts of the allusions. Esther 3:4 ("Day after day they spoke to him but he refused to comply") mirrors Genesis 39:10 ("And though she spoke to Joseph day after day, he refused to go to bed with her or even be with her"). The two texts depict Mordecai's refusal to bow and Joseph's refusal to sleep with Potiphar respectively. Yet Joseph's refusal to give in to the temptation is quite different than Mordecai's refusal to bow to Haman. One is clearly seen as a commitment to uphold God's will and the other less so. Esther 4:16 ("if I perish, I perish") reflects Genesis 43:14 ("If I am bereaved, I am bereaved"). Yet contextually there is a drastic contrast between (a) Esther's lack of confidence in God and his ability

Therefore, I affirm the conclusion of Ronald Pierce that "the author's omission of any reference to Deity in Esther actually serves to highlight the secular nature of the people of God in the ancient diaspora."[15] Similarly, F. B. Huey Jr. notes that the typical interpretation of Esther regarding God's activity behind the scenes "should be reexamined to see whether God's silence should be interpreted as evidence that the people were working out of their own affairs without consulting him."[16] He states elsewhere:

> I believe a profitable approach would be to see that the primary intent of the book is to show that the post-exilic people of Israel have not changed in spite of the punishment inflicted on them in the years following 587 B.C., [sic] a message more explicitly stated in the book of Malachi.[17]

The lingering effects of exile provide an adequate explanation for the assimilated character of the Jews in the story. The absence of God therefore functions as part of the continuing curses of the covenant. God's absence from the story is an indictment.[18]

But please do not misunderstand me; God *is* providentially involved in the story of Esther, but that is not *the point* of God's "absence" from the narrative. There is "coincidental" material in the story of Esther that seems to point to God's involvement. An example of this from elsewhere in the Old Testament is when an arrow struck Ahab "at random" piercing him

---

to deliver the Jews, and (b) the words of Israel/Jacob earlier in Genesis 43:14—"And may God Almighty grant you mercy before the man so that he will let your other brother and Benjamin come back with you." Israel refers unknowingly to Joseph ("the man") and shows a strong reliance on God in this scene, but such cannot be said for Esther and Mordecai. Esther 6:11 ("So Haman got the robe and the horse. He robed Mordecai, and led him on horseback through the city streets, proclaiming before him, 'This is what is done for the man the king delights to honor!'") alludes to Genesis 41:42–43 ("Then Pharaoh took his signet ring from his finger and put it on Joseph's finger. He dressed him in robes of fine linen and put a gold chain around his neck. He had him ride in a chariot as his second-in-command, and people shouted before him, 'Make way!' Thus he put him in charge of the whole land of Egypt"). Yet the important contrast is that Pharaoh elevates Joseph after recognizing the work of God in him (Gen 41:39–40). For more information on these allusions to the Joseph narrative and more, albeit with a different interpretation of their significance, see Berg, *Book of Esther*, 123–65.

15. Pierce, "Politics of Esther and Mordecai," 77.

16. Huey, "Esther," 787.

17. Huey, "Irony as Key," 38.

18. Isaiah speaks of God "hiding" his face as the result of sin (Isa 45:15a; 59:2b; 64:7) and Micah speaks of God's silence as a negative result (Mic 3:7).

between pieces of armor (1 Kgs 22:34), yet the text never states that God guided the arrow. The coincidence points beyond itself, however. The same is true in Esther. Yet the important thing to realize is that the characters do not recognize the "coincidences" in this way. Thus, we must distinguish between the characters and the author. And our author is winking at us.

How would an ancient reader have interpreted the multiple coincidences within the book of Esther? Would pre-Enlightenment readers have considered these to be merely chance occurrences? It is more likely that the earlier readers recognized the hand of God at work in the story of Esther, and that the author intended for this. To borrow an expression, it was believed that "a coincidence is a miracle in which God prefers to remain anonymous."[19] But we must maintain a distinction between (a) what was recognized by the readers and intended by the author, with (b) how the characters perceived these things within the narrative. We are not given any clue that the characters recognized these coincidences as providential acts of God. This is why conclusions such as those offered by Barry Webb are unwarranted—"the way the characters in the story behave, and the speeches they make at crucial points, clearly indicate *their* belief that something more than chance or purely natural causation is at work" (emphasis original).[20] Note also the similar principle that David Firth draws from the Esther narrative—"It is as God's people commit themselves to God's purposes that we discern his providence at work."[21] He states further:

> What is crucial here is that the coincidences happen when Mordecai and Esther have committed themselves to God and his people. But there is certainly a sense here that when God's people commit themselves to his purposes, as Esther and Mordecai have, then such coincidences are that much more frequent.[22]

Yet if these comments by Webb and Firth were correct why do we never read of Esther and Mordecai expressing certainty along these lines? Indeed, as I argued in chapters 1–2 of this study we have very little evidence at all for anything remotely religious about the Jewish identity of Mordecai and Esther. Rather we have plenty of reasons to assume that their lifestyles were assimilated with the surrounding Persian culture. In fact, the most likely place for religious conviction and confidence—Esther 4:1–17—has been

19. Levenson, *Esther*, 19.

20. Webb, *Five Festal Garments*, 121.

21. Firth, *Message of Esther*, 58.

22. Ibid., 99.

shown to communicate a very different picture of the beliefs and assumptions of the main characters than has often been thought. Thus, it is not the characters who see "more than chance or purely natural causation" at work, but rather it is the author who recognizes this and shows it to us obliquely so as to avoid distracting his readers from the secularity of the characters in the story.

The most important "coincidence" is the king's inability to sleep on the very night that Haman was preparing to kill Mordecai in Esther 6 (*wink wink*). Because of his unrest a courtier reads to him from the chronicles of the king's reign and it just so happened (*wink wink*) that the courtier read from the section about Mordecai thwarting the plot to kill the king (see 2:21–23), for which he had yet to be rewarded. This is *the* "coincidence" in Esther. Structurally, its importance cannot be missed. Esther 6 takes place on the night that separates the two feasts that Esther prepared for the king and Haman with the intent to overturn Haman's decree. See the figure below for the complete list of feasts:[23]

1	1:2–4	180 day feast for princes, noblemen, and military leaders
2	1:5–8	7 day feast for all people, from the least to the greatest
3	1:9	Vashti's feast for the women
4	2:18	The feast celebrating Esther's coronation as queen
5	3:15	The feast celebrating the edict to exterminate the Jews
6	5:6–8	Esther's first feast for Haman and the king[24]
7	7:1–9	Esther's second feast for Haman and the king
8	8:17	A feast celebrating Mordecai's promotion and the arrival of Mordecai's counter-edict
9	9:17	The feast celebrating Jewish victory throughout the provinces of Persia
10	9:18	The feast celebrating Jewish victory in Susa

23. See the similar chart in Fox, *Character and Ideology*, 157. Not everyone agrees that there are ten feasts in the story. Jobes, for example, only includes eight, omitting Vashti's feast (1:9) and the "feast" of Haman and the king after signing the edict to destroy the Jews (3:15). See Jobes, *Esther*, 155. Vashti's banquet is clearly a separate feast for the women and should therefore be included in the list of banquets. The "feast" of Haman and Mordecai (3:15) appears at first to be an unlikely "feast," but the verb used for drinking in the Hebrew (*šth*) contains the root word for the noun "feast" (*mišteh*) used in all the other examples. This is primarily because the main feature of the "feasts" was wine (see 1:7–8; 5:6; 7:2).

24. It may be that this banquet was intended for Haman. See McClure, "Esther's Banquet for Haman."

Thus, the key "coincidence" of the story occurs just before the climatic banquet in which Esther finally confronts Haman before the king (Esth 7), which is actually the seventh banquet mentioned in the story, providing an additional level of significance to it.[25]

In a book that provides the origin-story for the Festival of Purim, deriving its name from Haman casting lots (*pur*),[26] it should be no surprise that there are "coincidences" in the story. It is important to realize that casting lots was not a game of chance; it was the exact opposite. Casting lots was meant to reveal what had already been determined. Thus, casting lots is about fate and predetermination. Hence the "coincidences" play off the whole notion of divine involvement in human affairs. On the day that Haman had originally set out to destroy the Jews, the day the lots had indicated, we are told that "the reverse occurred" (Esth 9:1). Haman's lots however did in fact indicate the time of decisive victory, but it was for the Jews and not for Haman. This is reminiscent of a scene from the historian Herodotus who records an oracle received by King Croesus of Lydia saying that "he would destroy a great empire" if he attacked Persia (*Histories*, 1.53). After depicting the subsequent downfall of King Croesus, Herodotus writes, "The oracle was fulfilled; Croesus has destroyed a mighty empire—his own" (*Histories*, 1.86). As Scripture attests, God thwarts the crafty (Job 5:12). "The lot is cast into the lap," the proverb states, "but its every decision is from the LORD" (Prov 16:33). No matter what mortal plans are made, "it is the LORD's purpose that prevails" (Prov 19:21). Haman cast his lots the day before Passover (Esth 3:12), and even though the God of Purim was not celebrated to be so, he proved that he was still the God of the exodus.

The deliverance of the Jews at the end of the story of Esther, without minimizing the problems of the story (see chapters 1–2), is therefore to be seen as God's deliverance of his people even though they do not recognize it or perceive it as such. The God who is faithful to his unfaithful people is the elusive God of Esther.

---

25. There may be additional levels of significance here as well. Levenson suggests that Esther 6 is the middle section of a larger chiastic structure (see Levenson, *Esther*, 8). Also, since Esther 4 marks the beginning of the Feast of Passover (see 3:12) and Esther fasted for "three days" (4:16—5:1), this would mean that the night that the king was unable to sleep would have been during the seven-day celebration of Passover. This opens up the possibility that the author may be playing off the Passover context further, since Exod 12:42 speaks of a "night of watching" (so Berlin, *Esther*, xxxvii).

26. A possibly relevant text for background on Purim is *The Die (pūru) of Yaḫali* (2.113i in Hallo and Younger, *Context of Scripture*).

Canonical Perspectives

How then does this message of God's faithfulness to an unfaithful people cohere with the biblical message and present itself as applicable and relevant for the church today? In our attempt to situate Esther within a broader theological framework we must avoid a major potential pitfall. I have in mind the attempt to turn Esther into an allegory for the church.

Avoid Christian Allegories

Two explicit examples of allegorizing the story of Esther come from Samuel Wells and Michael Beckett respectively. In Wells's commentary, he offers a discussion on Esther as *a type of Christ*, suggesting that there is an insight about the nature of the incarnation in the story of Esther. Since Esther becomes queen before Haman's hostility is revealed, Wells somehow sees in this a pattern that undercuts the typical theological paradigm of "creation-fall-covenant-incarnation" because "in the book of Esther the incarnation precedes the fall."[27] Then he states further, "The christological illumination of this is to give weight to the conviction that the incarnation is not simply God's response to humanity's fall, but is a part of the overflowing and manifestation of God's very nature; in other words, there would have been an incarnation had there been no fall."[28]

Beckett suggests similarly that "Esther represents a female Christ figure."[29] This representation, according to Beckett, has "huge implications" for the debate about "female priesthood."[30] Whatever we might make of the role of women within church ministry, surely Esther does not help us answer that question. Additionally, Beckett makes Esther a type of David[31] (even though she was a descendent of King Saul), and speaks of her as also representing every human as "the second Adam."[32] Somehow Beckett is able to extend this allegorical interpretation into a vision of universalism and the salvation of all people through the fact that Mordecai's edict

27. Wells and Sumner, *Esther & Daniel*, 16.
28. Ibid., 17. See also ibid., 45–46.
29. Beckett, *Gospel in Esther*, 7.
30. Ibid.
31. Ibid., 17.
32. Ibid., 29–30.

(8:8–14) functions to counteract Haman's initial edict (3:12–15).[33] Beckett asserts, "God will deliver (save) all his people—the separatist remnant and the accommodated non-returnees, the religious and the secular, the Jew and the Gentile—for he has committed himself in his covenant to the deliverance of, [sic] the re-establishing of a relationship with the blessing of all humankind."[34] Beckett's typology/allegory clearly misses the point. Esther does not show us how God is gracious to everyone, but rather to his people (even those who are unfaithful). We simply cannot extrapolate a soteriological universalism from this story—Haman, his ten sons, and the other 75,800 dead will not let us.

The Effect of Canonical Order(s)

So if we can avoid these sorts of allegorical pitfalls, we can see that the Hebrew story of Esther on its own terms offers some rich theological connections with the overall message of the Bible. As we are in the process of teasing out how precisely Esther *fits* within the canon of the church's Scripture, having concluded in the previous chapter that Esther does indeed *belong* in the canon, it is important to consider Esther's *placement* in the canonical order. The ordering of biblical books has an important hermeneutical contribution for those reading through various books of the Bible. Whether we recognize it or not, the canonical shape affects our reading of individual books and conditions us to read them a certain way. So an interesting question to ask is, how did the compilers of canonical lists make their decisions? Although it may be relevant to consider to what degree the author of Esther was conscious of its possible inclusion within a set of "canonical" or authoritative literature (see Esth 9:20–32), our primary concern is to recognize that the act of organizing Esther within a larger collection (i.e., the canon) *at a particular location in the order of that collection* is itself an act of interpretation on the part of the organizer or canonizer. So we want to consider both (a) how Esther's placement in the canonical order affects readers, and (b) how the organization represents an interpretation of Esther. We will begin with the effect on readers.

For illustrative purposes, consider a couple analogies for the way canonical shaping impacts the reader. The first example is from the beloved seven-part fictional tale by C. S. Lewis, *The Chronicles of Narnia*. Since the

33. Ibid., 122.
34. Ibid., 127.

books were written out of chronological order, two different orderings for the seven books have been suggested. Are the books to be read in the order in which they were written or should the books be arranged according to the chronology internal to the books? See the figure below:

Publication Order	Storyline Chronology[35]
The Lion, the Witch and the Wardrobe (1950)	*The Magician's Nephew*
Prince Caspian (1951)	*The Lion, the Witch and the Wardrobe*
The Voyage of the Dawn Treader (1952)	*The Horse and His Boy*
The Silver Chair (1953)	*Prince Caspian*
The Horse and His Boy (1954)	*The Voyage of the Dawn Treader*
The Magician's Nephew (1955)	*The Silver Chair*
The Last Battle (1956)	*The Last Battle*

If you enjoy the fiction of C. S. Lewis you probably have your own opinion on this topic. The point of the illustration is not to argue that one is right and the other is wrong. In fact, C. S. Lewis wrote a letter in response to a young fan's eager request to know the proper reading order, saying, "perhaps it does not matter very much in what order anyone reads them."[36] So rather than trying to show that one canonical order is preferable to another, I merely want to note how the arrangement affects the reader. If one is introduced to the world of Narnia in *The Magician's Nephew* the reader experiences Narnia first through a Genesis-like story about the creation of Narnia. Yet this book was actually written sixth out of seven and can also function as a flashback, being the penultimate tale before the climatic end of the series. However, if one experiences Narnia for the first time the same way the Pevensie children do, such a reader is pulled into the same wonder that the children experience, not knowing how Narnia came to be, but nevertheless marveling that it *is*.[37]

The second example for illustrative purposes comes from *Star Wars*. Similar to *The Chronicles of Narnia*, the six *Star Wars* films were made out of chronological sequence.[38] The "original trilogy"—*Episode IV: A New*

35. This order has been maintained by HarperCollins.

36. Edwards, *Further Up & Further In*, xi, citing Dorsett and Mead, *C. S. Lewis Letters to Children*, 68–69.

37. See Edwards, *Further Up & Further In*, viii–xi.

38. At the time of my writing, Disney has announced that there will be a seventh *Star Wars* film (with the intent to make more). This further demonstrates the point being

Hope; Episode V: The Empire Strikes Back; Episode VI: Return of the Jedi—
was made in the late 1970s and early 1980s. Then the three subsequent
movies that comprise the "prequel trilogy"—*Episode I: The Phantom Men-
ace; Episode II: Attack of the Clones; Episode III: Revenge of the Sith*—were
made from 1999 to 2005, all taking place chronologically before *Episode
IV: A New Hope*. With the "prequel trilogy" of *Star Wars* being released
years after the "original trilogy" this created an issue for the proper order in
which viewers should watch the movies. Does the "prequel trilogy" function as a flashback and back-story to be watched after one has already seen
the "original trilogy" (creating the order IV, V, VI, I, II, III), or is the viewer
meant to start with the "prequel trilogy" and then proceed to the "original
trilogy" (creating the order I, II, III, IV, V, VI)? It was ostensibly the intention of creator George Lucas from the very beginning that the proper order
for viewing the series begins with *Episode I* and proceeds through *Episode
VI*. Yet if viewers follow this (admittedly intuitive) order there is a tragic
cinematic price to be paid. One of the most significant twists in film history
is completely jeopardized—the revelation at the climax of *Episode V: The
Empire Strikes Back* (*spoiler alert!*) that Darth Vader is the father of Luke
Skywalker. The importance of that moment for the story arc of the "original trilogy," the entire *Star Wars* saga more broadly, and even film history
in general, should not be underestimated. If one begins with the "prequel
trilogy," it is made quite plain that Luke is the son of Anakin Skywalker,
the Jedi who turns to the Dark Side and becomes Darth Vader and so the
impact of the twist is lost. The point here is not that there is a right or wrong
order to watching *Star Wars*, but simply that the order has a clear impact
on the experience.

A similar effect happens with the canonical order of the books of
the Bible.[39] I will comment first on the New Testament since each of the
major Christian traditions—Catholic, Orthodox, Protestant—has the
same twenty-seven books in exactly the same canonical order. The New
Testament places the Gospels up front, showing the obvious importance
attributed to Jesus. The decision to move Acts away from its counterpart
(Luke) was likely because of an intention to keep the three similar Gospels
(the "Synoptics"; Matthew, Mark, and Luke) together along with the Gospel

---

made about telling stories out of chronological sequence (i.e., IV, V, VI, I, II, III, VII . . .).

39. For interesting discussions on this, see Goswell, "Order of the Books in the Hebrew Bible," 673–88; *idem*, "Order of the Books in the Greek Old Testament," 449–66;
idem, "Order of the Books in the New Testament," 225–41.

of John. Acts then functions as a canonical transition into the writings of Paul, whose ministry is described in Acts 9–28. Naturally then, the book of Acts has been utilized to develop a "Pauline chronology" in relation to his letters. After Paul's letters the canon transitions into the other epistles, the "catholic epistles" or "general letters," as they are sometimes called because of their broader intended audiences. Finally, the New Testament concludes appropriately with the book of Revelation and its vision of new heavens and a new earth (Rev 21–22), providing a fitting bookend to the Bible regarding creation's restoration in relation to the corruption of creation in Genesis 1–3. These bookends themselves contribute to the canonical shape of the Bible and our interpretation of it.

Since the order of Old Testament books varies between Protestant and Jewish orderings, we will take a look at both. Before doing so it should be noted that none of the orders described here are "right" or "wrong." Yet it would be mistaken to assume that the orders are therefore irrelevant. We will see how in each case the order affects the reader and witnesses to certain intentions on the part of those organizing the collection.

In regards to one ordering of the Hebrew Scriptures (the *BHS*; following the Leningrad Codex), the book of Ruth was placed directly after the book of Proverbs. This means that the transition from the beloved woman extolled in Proverbs 31 to the character of Ruth offers interpretive connections for the reader and points to the organizing rationale. In the Protestant canon Ruth is placed between Judges and 1 Samuel. This placement connects Ruth to the era of Israel's Judges, as Ruth 1:1 attests to, and the end of Ruth (4:16–22) anticipates the story of David with the birth of Obed, David's ancestor. Thus, the end of Ruth functions as a nice transition into 1 Samuel and the life of David.

Many other examples of this could be noted but the point is to comment on Esther's placement within the canon. In Jewish orderings (*BHS* and *JPS*), Esther is placed beside Daniel. The two books overlap in several ways, but what becomes apparent is the juxtaposition between two very different responses to life in the pagan palace, and ultimately, to exile. Daniel and his three friends refused to be defiled by the king's royal food (Dan 1:8–21) and show constant assurance and dependence on God throughout, whether it is in the face of the fiery furnace (Dan 3) or in the midst of the lion's den (Dan 6).[40] Esther and Mordecai, however, conceal their identity,

---

40. This is contrary to what is depicted in Gini Andrews's novel, *Esther: The Star and the Sceptre*, where Mordecai consoles Esther as she considers the king's decree by reminding her about the story of Shadrach, Meshach, and Abednego from Daniel 3. When

have forgotten the promises of God, and show no concern about keeping his laws. With the canonical light of Daniel cast upon the story of Esther the darkness is exposed.

In the Protestant order Esther is placed just after Ezra and Nehemiah. These two books take place in the same post-exilic Persian context yet reflect the strongest disdain against assimilation in the whole Bible.[41] Try reading Ezra, Nehemiah, and Esther in one sitting; the contrasts are staggering. On the other side of Esther is Job. This is interesting because Job is a story wrestling with the age-old question, "why do bad things happen to good people?" Thus, we see Esther as a tale of how *good things happen to undeserving people*. Job's friends suppose that he must have done something egregious or else God would not be punishing him. The same sort of reflection takes place in Esther, but in reverse. The theology of Job's friends is divine retribution. This is essentially the theology of Deuteronomy— blessings for obedience, curses for disobedience—and that represented in the so-called "Deuteronomistic history" (Joshua, Judges, 1–2 Samuel, 1–2 Kings). Thus, the friends of Job were speaking with a certain biblical intuition. Yet the problem that the friends of Job had was assuming that God is mechanical. Even at the end, when God finally appeared (Job 38–41), he did not clarify the nature of divine retribution, rather he qualified it ("were you there?"). The story of Job is an exception, and the story of Esther is another kind of exception.

Esther in Canonical Concert

Now that we have seen Esther's placement in its immediate canonical context(s), let us hear the song of Esther in concert with the whole Bible. Viewing Esther as a depiction of God's faithfulness to his unfaithful people is ultimately about God's original promise to Abraham (then Abram)— "I will bless those who bless you, and whoever curses you I will curse" (Gen 12:3; see also Num 24:9). When God promised Abraham a large offspring, as large as the stars in the sky (Gen 15:5), God took it upon himself to fulfill the terms of the covenant unilaterally, demonstrating this by passing through the split animal parts as Abraham lay passive and un-attentive in a deep sleep (Gen 15:17). When this covenantal background to Esther is

---

Esther recalls that there was a 'fourth figure' in the fiery furnace, Mordecai tells her, "That same fourth figure, my Hadassah, will go with you into the palace" (Andrews, *Esther*, 78).

41. See pp. 27–28 from chapter 1.

recognized we can see that if Haman was successful and all the Jews were destroyed, *God would have been unfaithful to his promise.* This original promise of preservation is reiterated throughout Scripture, as it reads in 2 Kings, "And since the LORD had not said he would blot out the name of Israel from under heaven, he saved them" (2 Kgs 14:27), and as God promised through the prophet Jeremiah, "I will not completely destroy you" (Jer 46:28b). God's commitment to preserve Israel as he promised is ultimately for his own sake, not for theirs—"It is not for your sake, people of Israel, that I am going to do these things, but for the sake of my holy name, which you have profaned among the nations where you have gone" (Ezek 36:22). Even though God's name was profaned among the nations during the exile, God still preserved his people. Thus, God upheld his holy name, his righteousness, and his faithfulness by delivering his unfaithful people.

God's promise to preserve his people, even after sending them into exile, is remarkable because the exilic community could never have merited any future deliverance from God, nor could they make atonement through sacrifices since the temple was destroyed and they were so far removed from Jerusalem. If Israel was to be delivered from exile, God would have to act to redeem an unfaithful people, and in this way God would remain faithful to his promises, and ultimately to himself. As God's promise recorded in Leviticus states, "when they are in the land of their enemies, I will not reject them or abhor them so as to destroy them completely, breaking my covenant with them" (Lev 26:44). Likewise, as the psalmist says about God, "he does not treat us as our sins deserve" (Ps 103:10). Surely if he did there would be no deliverance, for anyone. Note the words of Psalm 78 and Psalm 106 and how they reflect God's continual faithfulness despite his people's unfaithfulness:

> Their hearts were not loyal to him,
> they were not faithful to his covenant.
> Yet he was merciful;
> he forgave their iniquities
> and did not destroy them.
> Time after time he restrained his anger
> and did not stir up his full wrath.
> He remembered that they were but flesh,
> a passing breeze that does not return. (Psalm 78:37–39)

> We have sinned, even as our ancestors did;
> we have done wrong and acted wickedly.
> When our ancestors were in Egypt,

> they gave no thought to your miracles;
> they did not remember your many kindnesses,
> and they rebelled by the sea, the Red Sea.
> Yet he saved them for his name's sake,
> to make his mighty power known. (Psalm 106:6–8)

Note how this theology is articulated in Isaiah as well. Isaiah speaks of the exilic community's disregard for God in exile, "Yet you have not called on me, Jacob, you have not wearied yourselves for me, Israel. You have not brought me sheep for burnt offerings, nor honored me with your sacrifices" (Isa 43:22–23a). Despite the lack of faithfulness on the part of the exiles *in exile*, the Lord declared, "I, even, I, am he who blots out your transgressions, for my own sake, and remembers your sins no more" (Isa 43:25). This all leads directly into a promise that Israel will return to the land and be restored (Isa 44:1–5). Note further these two additional texts from Isaiah:

> Well do I know how treacherous you are; you were called a rebel from birth. For my own name's sake I delay my wrath; for the sake of my praise I hold it back from you, so as not to destroy you completely. See, I have refined you, though not as silver; I have tested you in the furnace of affliction. For my own sake, for my own sake, I do this. How can I let myself be defamed? I will not yield my glory to another (Isa 48:8b–11).

> "I will not accuse them forever, nor will I always be angry, for then they would faint away because of me—the very people I have created. I was enraged by their sinful greed; I punished them, and hid my face in anger, yet they kept on in their willful ways. I have seen their ways, but I will heal them; I will guide them and restore comfort to Israel's mourners, creating praise on their lips. Peace, peace, to those far and near," says the LORD. "And I will heal them." (Isa 57:16–19).

These promises were no doubt viewed as great signs of mercy to the exilic communities. Eventually the early Christians saw in these promises to Israel-in-exile a way to understand God's embrace of the nations as well. This pattern of interpretation can be seen especially in the writings of the Apostle Paul, who applied Old Testament texts, which were originally spoken to Israel when she was scattered throughout the nations, to those very nations themselves (see Rom 9:25–26; 2 Cor 6:16–18; Gal 4:21–31). David Starling[42] has conducted an important study on this feature of Pauline

---

42. Starling, *Not My People*.

hermeneutics that sheds additional light on how the church can further embrace Esther as Christian Scripture.

It is well known that Paul was the Apostle to the Gentiles (see Acts 9; 1 Cor 9; Eph 3:1–6; 2 Cor 3) and his life and ministry was devoted to extending the blessings and promises of Israel's God to the nations. Yet it has often been wondered how Paul can get away with the hermeneutical moves involved in applying texts meant for Israel-in-exile to Gentiles. This is where Starling's work is so helpful. He has shown, rightly in my opinion, how Paul's assumptions about Israel's exile and the Gentile nations coalesce and provide insight into how Paul believed that Gentiles could be embraced by Israel's God. It was precisely because God embraced Israel-in-exile, that is to say, Israel in the position of experiencing the curses of the covenant, that God could then likewise embrace the Gentiles (i.e., those outside the covenant). Thus, when we as Christians read the story of Esther in all of its proper secularity, we find God's embrace of a people assimilated to their pagan context as a result of the exile and those continuing to experience the absence of God as an extension of the covenantal curses. Thus, in Esther we see God embrace Israel-in-exile—those experiencing not the blessings of the covenant but curses, those who had been unfaithful—and all of this ultimately prefigures God's embrace of the nations. Because God can embrace Israel-in-exile he can also embrace those from the lands of exile. As Paul wrote in Ephesians 2:17, utilizing the Isaianic promise noted above about Israel-in-exile from Isaiah 57:19 as a message of comfort to the Gentiles, "He came and preached peace to you who were far away and peace to those who were near" (Eph 2:17).[43]

Esther's message of God's embrace of his unfaithful people culminates in God's embrace of the Messiah Jesus who bore the full weight of Israel's exile on the cross,[44] experiencing profoundly the absence of God—"*My God, my God, why have you forsaken me?*" (Mk 15:34)—the ultimate curse of exile. Yet God vindicated the Messiah, the one who *became our unfaithfulness* (2 Cor 5:21), by providing the ultimate return from exile in the resurrection from the dead.[45] Since no one deserves to be vindicated on their own (Rom 3:9–18), all who identify with the Messiah—all the unfaithful people who

---

43. As Starling (*Not My People*, 193) notes on this passage, "Gentiles can find themselves addressed in a promise originally given to exiled Israelites because the predicament of exile which the promises addressed correspond so precisely with their own predicament as Gentiles, spiritually dead and far off from God."

44. So Wright, *Jesus and the Victory of God*, 594–97.

45. See resurrection imagery as a metaphor for the return from exile in Ezekiel 37.

turn to identify with *the Unfaithful One*—will likewise be vindicated, both Jews and Gentiles, both Israel-in-exile and the nations of the exile.

Conclusion & Summary

The perspective of this book taken as a whole is that Esther is a story about how God was faithful to an unfaithful people. This is how a secular story functions as Scripture. Thus, when the church seeks to appropriate Esther for teaching and preaching, the urge to amplify the story of Esther by making the characters religious paragons, as seen in the ancient translations and modern popular versions, should be resisted. The Bible is full of stories with heroes and protagonists that the church should not seek to emulate, and Esther is no exception. Though as we have seen, the secularity of the characters should be distinguished from the perspective of the author, who has chosen to recall Israel's deliverance in a highly ironic and self-critical manner.

It is therefore a mistake to assume, as many have, that God was responding to the actions of his people in the story of Esther. Note the words of Joan Wolf, author of *A Reluctant Queen*, in an authorial note at the end of her novel:

> Where the Bible story and the novel come together is in the underlying premise. God has a plan for the world, and He works His plan through the actions of humans. The big question is, will we allow God to work through us? God wants us to be His partners, but we have free will to accept or refuse His challenge. In the Judeo-Christian tradition, all of God's people must listen to His voice and open their hearts for Him to use us for His purposes.[46]

However, these ideas find no connection to the story of Esther as I have tried to demonstrate. God was responding *despite* the actions of his people. The absence of direct reference to God and religious customs in the narrative highlights this fact. God was not summoned or invoked through either prayer or repentance; he freely acted. This was entirely due to his faithfulness to his people—a unilateral and unconditional faithfulness to his covenantal promises.

It must be made clear, however, that the message of God's faithfulness to his unfaithful people in Esther is not meant to open the door for the

---

46. Wolf, *Reluctant Queen*, 375.

church to live however she wants, or to permit licentiousness. The story of Esther is a tribute to God's freedom, as well as his commitment to keep his people from total annihilation. One must not miss the salvation-historical nature of the interpretation being offered here. The deliverance in Esther is not eschatological deliverance; thus we cannot see a pattern of God "saving" those who remain unrepentantly unfaithful. Esther is about the preservation of God's people as a whole; it is a testament to the fact that God will not ultimately disown his covenant people or let them be completely destroyed. Jesus's promise to the church that the gates of Hell will never prevail against her (Matt 16:18) can be seen as an extension of this promise. When we look at the history of the Christian church we can see instances of unfaithfulness yet God continued to guide and direct. However, God's patience is not to be tried, nor his mercy taken for granted. Esther's elusive God is at once the covenant God and the free God, capable of showing mercy and grace to the undeserving.

A Closer Look at the Relationship between the LXX and the AT

In chapter 3 (*Esther & the Cover-Up*) we saw how expansive the Greek translations are. Yet explaining the relationship between the two translations, the Septuagint (LXX) and the Alpha-Text (AT), has been relegated to the present appendix. There are multiple issues to address in this debate, but my primary goal is simply to demonstrate *that all religious material in the Greek translations is secondary*. In keeping with the perspective of this book, the appendix is meant to buttress the argument that the author of the Hebrew story of Esther intentionally avoided religious imagery and theology in order to highlight the secularity and assimilation of the protagonists. What we will see here is that regardless of how one understands the origins of the story, religious elements were added later rather than earlier.

The basic problem with the Greek translations that has sparked all the debate is threefold. (1) When the LXX and the AT are compared side by side it is apparent that the AT is much shorter (by roughly 20 percent)[1]; (2) both the LXX and the AT contain all six of the Additions (A–F)[2] but with some variation; and (3) the majority of the differences occur in the body of the text. So the fact that the AT is quite shorter *in the body* and yet contains the same six Additions as the LXX has incited much scholarly debate.

It is not necessary to go into too much detail here, but suffice it to say that there are essentially two basic ways to explain the divergence (naturally with multiple nuances here and there). The first position suggests that the

1. See Jobes, *Alpha-Text of Esther*, 147.
2. Ibid., 162.

body of the AT, minus the six Additions, is a translation of an independent Hebrew text that was different from the Hebrew version we know (the Masoretic Text; or MT).[3] According to this position, the six major Additions were either acquired from the LXX, or somewhere else, at a later stage. Thus, scholars who advocate this position speak of a "proto-AT" when referring to the AT without the Additions, which is a way of speaking about an earlier version of the Hebrew story. This view, with unique alterations by each scholar, has been defended by C. A. Moore,[4] D. J. A. Clines,[5] M. V. Fox,[6] and K. H. Jobes,[7] among others. On the other side of the scholarly divide is the position that there was no such thing as a "proto-AT" and therefore no independent Hebrew tradition to which the AT attests. Rather, the AT is a *recension* of the LXX, meaning that the AT was an intentional revision of the LXX, and was therefore composed after the LXX. This is the position advocated by K. De Troyer,[8] R. Hanhart,[9] and others. Below is a figure comparing the two positions using De Troyer and Fox as representatives for each:[10]

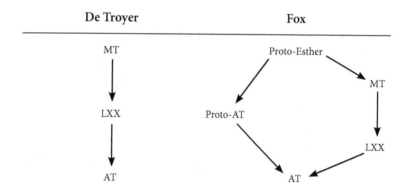

3. I will refer to the Hebrew text as the MT knowing full well that such a designation in this context is anachronistic. I use it so that readers will not be bogged down by designations like "proto-MT" to refer to the Hebrew consonants without the Masoretic pointing.

4. C. Moore, *Esther*; idem, *Daniel, Esther, and Jeremiah*.

5. Clines, *Esther Scroll*.

6. Fox, *Redaction of the Books of Esther*.

7. Jobes, *Alpha-Text of Esther*.

8. De Troyer, *End of the Alpha Text of Esther*.

9. Hanhart, *Esther*.

10. These charts are slightly modified from the ones found in Fox (*Redaction of the Books of Esther*, 9) and De Troyer (*End of the Alpha Text of Esther*, 39).

As is apparent, the position of De Troyer is a simpler reconstruction. The Hebrew text (MT) was modified by the LXX, which was then subjected to a literary revision that produced the AT. Fox's position is a little more complicated. For him, the "proto-AT" (which is, once again, the AT without the six Additions) reflects a unique Hebrew tradition independent from the MT and therefore suggests that there was an even earlier version of the Esther story that influenced both traditions, designated as "proto-Esther." The AT then came into its present shape through the influence of the LXX (mostly in the Additions, though not exclusively so).

If De Troyer is correct then our arguments for the secondary nature of the religious imagery are justified. However, in the case of Fox's reconstruction, and others who hold a similar view, it is necessary to consider the possibility that the religious imagery was present in the story at the early stage he calls "proto-Esther." So, we are left with two options: either the Hebrew version (MT) excised the religious imagery, or the "proto-AT" added it along the way. Thus, for the rest of this brief appendix our concern will be on how to navigate the possibility of Fox's reconstruction being true.

If Fox is correct about the existence of the hypothetical "proto-Esther," this would mean that the Hebrew story that we know today was a development in its own right. How then should we think about our Esther story being a development of an earlier version? Consider an example from the Gospel of Luke. The Gospel begins with a statement that Luke utilized multiple sources and testimonies for the compilation of his Gospel (Luke 1:1–4). In fact, most scholars believe that Luke utilized the Gospel of Mark as one of his sources (possibly even the hypothetical "Q" source, which is the material shared by Matthew and Luke not found in Mark). Along with oral tradition and eyewitness testimony, we can imagine that Luke had quite a bit at his disposal for the composition of his Gospel. Just as there were earlier forms and stages in the development of Luke's Gospel, it could have happened similarly with the story of Esther. So it is entirely possible that the Esther story was indeed a development of an earlier version. However, it is not necessary for us to conclude with Fox that there was such a thing as a "proto-Esther" for the purposes of this study. The main concern is whether or not the Hebrew version (MT) would have removed religious imagery from the earlier versions.

Since "proto-AT" contains religious imagery—the AT as a whole appears to have more references to God than the LXX[11]—and the Hebrew

---

11. De Troyer and Schulte, "Is God Absent or Present," 37.

Appendix

story (MT) does not contain the same imagery, we have to explain why this is the case. Does the "proto-AT" then reflect the source it was translating accurately in regards to religious imagery, or was this imagery inserted along the way at some point? The reason why this question is important is because it determines whether the MT was consistent with its source in not including religious imagery, or if the MT reflects a unique attempt to omit the religious imagery found in the earlier source.

D. J. A. Clines argues for the latter, proposing that "the MT represents a deliberate excision of *all* religious language."[12] He does not offer any reason why the author would *omit* religious reference systematically and it appears that he presumes the author felt the imagery was superfluous. He states, "Removal of explicitly religious language does not conceal divine causality, not if the holes that are left are God-shaped."[13] Levenson agrees, "The reason for the change would seem to be the MT's adherence to a subtle and demanding theology in which religious meaning is not manifest in human actions but lies behind them."[14] However, it is one thing to suggest that the author deliberately avoided religious imagery (as I suggest), but it is a much more difficult thing to demonstrate why an author would attempt to remove all religious imagery from an earlier tradition that contained it.[15] It seems much more likely that (a) whatever we make of earlier versions of the story, the author of the MT was telling the story without religious imagery because the story *did not contain religious imagery originally*, and (b) religious additions to the story, of all stripes, represent alterations done to the text. So I reckon, if there was a "proto-AT," it was either (1) a translation of an *expansive tradition* from an earlier Hebrew source, or (2) an *expansive translation* of a Hebrew tradition that was similar to the MT in regards to nonreligious imagery. Take a look at the figure below for an example of a clear expansion in the AT:

12. Clines, *Esther Scroll*, 109; cf. 112.

13. Ibid., 153.

14. Levenson, *Esther*, 33.

15. So also rightly Fox, *Redaction of the Books of Esther*, 120; Bush, *Ruth, Esther*, 291; De Troyer and Schulte, "Is God Absent or Present," 37–38.

MT (Esther 6:11 NRSV)	LXX (Esther 6:11 NRSV)	AT (Esther 7:14–19)[15]
So Haman took the robes and the horse and robed Mordecai and led him riding through the open square of the city, proclaiming, "Thus shall it be done for the man whom the king wishes to honor!"	So Haman got the robe and the horse; he put the robe on Mordecai and made him ride through the open square of the city, proclaiming, "Thus shall it be done to everyone whom the king wishes to honor."	And Haman took the robe and the horse, doing reverence to Mordecai even as on that very day he had determined to hang him. And he said to Mordecai, "Take off the sackcloth." Mordecai was troubled, as one who is dying, and in distress he put off the sackcloth and put on the garments of glory. And Mordecai thought he saw a portent; and his heart was toward the Lord; and he became speechless. Haman hastened to mount him upon the horse. And Haman led the horse outside, and brought him outside, proclaiming, "Thus shall be done for the man who fears the king, whom the king wishes to honour."

What is a rather simple verse with very little detail has become much more dramatically compelling and, in so doing, the ambiguous aspects of the text are clarified. No doubt a scribe would have wondered what happened to Mordecai's original lament garments and what Mordecai thought about being paraded around town and therefore chose to add these bits. Of course, we see a religious expansion of this scene as well in regards to the heavenly portent that Mordecai sees and identifies as a sign from the Lord. This expansion demonstrates that the AT is itself either an expansion of "Proto-Esther" (because it makes little sense that the Hebrew [MT] would shorten the details here) or it is subsequent to both the MT and LXX, and this example would represent some of the unique alterations done to the story.

---

16. Clines's translation, in *Esther Scroll*, 237.

Thus, I suggest that whatever we make of "Proto-Esther," the earliest Esther traditions did not have religious imagery and at no point in the transmission of the story was God ever excised; rather, if Fox is right in his reconstruction there are instead multiple attestations to religious elaborations to the story of Esther—"proto-AT," AT, the LXX without Additions, Addition A, Addition C, Addition D, Addition E, and Addition F.[17]

17. Addition B, although expansive, does not contain religious imagery.

Bibliography

Allen, Leslie C., and Timothy S. Laniak. *Ezra, Nehemiah, Esther*. New International Biblical Commentary. Peabody, MA: Hendrickson, 2003.

Anderson, Bernhard W. "The Place of the Book of Esther in the Christian Bible." *Journal of Religion* 30 (1950) 32–43.

Anderson, Gary A. *A Time to Mourn, a Time to Dance: The Expression of Grief and Joy in Israelite Religion*. University Park: Pennsylvania State University Press, 1991.

Andrews, Gini. *Esther: The Star and the Sceptre*. Grand Rapids: Zondervan, 1980.

Animated Stories from the Bible: Esther. DVD. Directed by Richard Rich. Burbank, CA: Rich Animation, 1993.

Baldwin, Joyce G. *Esther: An Introduction and Commentary*. Tyndale Old Testament Commentaries. Downers Grove, IL: InterVarsity, 1984.

Barnes, Albert. "Esther." In *Barnes' Notes*, edited by F. C. Cook, 2:487–504. Grand Rapids: Baker, 2001.

Barth, Karl. *Church Dogmatics*. 14 volumes. Peabody, MA: Hendrickson, 2010.

Bechtel, Carol M. *Esther*. Interpretation. Louisville: Westminster John Knox, 2002.

Beckett, Michael. *Gospel in Esther*. Carlisle, PA: Paternoster, 2002.

Beckwith, Roger T. "Formation of the Hebrew Bible." In *Mikra: Text, Translation, Reading, and Interpretation of the Hebrew Bible in Ancient Judaism and Early Christianity*, edited by Martin Jan Mulder, 39–86. Philadelphia: Fortress, 1988.

Berg, Sandra Beth. *The Book of Esther: Motifs, Themes, and Structure*. Society of Biblical Literature Dissertation Series 44. Missoula, MT: Scholars, 1979.

Berkhof, Louis. *Systematic Theology*. New ed. Grand Rapids: Eerdmans, 1996.

Berlin, Adele. *Esther = [Ester]: The Traditional Hebrew Text with the New JPS Translation*. Philadelphia: Jewish Publication Society, 2001.

Berlin, Adele, and Marc Zvi Brettler, eds. *The Jewish Study Bible: Jewish Publication Society Tanakh Translation*. Oxford: Oxford University Press, 1999.

The Bible: Esther. DVD. Directed by Raffaele Mertes. Munich: Beta, 1998.

Bickerman, Elias J. *Four Strange Books of the Bible: Jonah, Daniel, Koheleth, Esther*. New York: Schocken, 1967.

Bjornard, Reidar B. "Esther." In *Broadman Bible Commentary*, edited by Clifton J. Allen, 4:1–21. Nashville: Broadman, 1971.

Blomberg, Craig. "Matthew." In *Commentary on the New Testament Use of the Old Testament*, edited by G. K. Beale and D. A. Carson, 1–109. Grand Rapids: Baker, 2008.

The Book of Esther. DVD. Directed by David A. R. White. Scottsdale, AZ: Pure Flix, 2013.

Breneman, Mervin. *Ezra, Nehemiah, Esther*. New American Commentary. Nashville: Broadman & Holman, 1993.

Brown, David. *The Divine Trinity*. LaSalle, IL: Open Court, 1985.

Bush, Frederic W. *Ruth, Esther*. Word Biblical Commentary 9. Dallas: Word, 1996.

Calvin, John. *Institutes of the Christian Religion.* Translated by Henry Beveridge. Peabody, MA: Hendrickson, 2007.

Carruthers, Jo. *Esther through the Centuries.* Blackwell Bible Commentaries. Oxford: Blackwell, 2008.

Childs, Brevard S. *Biblical Theology of the Old and New Testaments: Theological Reflection on the Christian Bible.* London: SCM, 1992.

————. *Introduction to the Old Testament as Scripture.* London: SCM, 1979.

Clines, David J. A. *The Esther Scroll: The Story of the Story.* Journal for the Study of the Old Testament Supplement Series 30. Sheffield, UK: JSOT, 1984.

Conti, Marco, and Gianluca Pilara, eds. *1–2 Kings, 1–2 Chronicles, Ezra, Nehemiah, Esther.* Ancient Christian Commentary on Scripture, Old Testament 5. Downers Grove, IL: InterVarsity, 2008.

Craig, Kenneth M. *Reading Esther: A Case for the Literary Carnivalesque.* Literary Currents in Biblical Interpretation. Louisville: Westminster John Knox, 1995.

Crawford, Sidnie Ann White. "Esther." In *Women's Bible Commentary,* edited by Carol A. Newsom and Sharon H. Ringe, 124–29. Louisville: Westminster John Knox, 1998.

Day, Linda. *Esther.* Abingdon Old Testament Commentaries. Nashville: Abingdon, 2005.

De Troyer, Kristin. *The End of the Alpha Text of Esther: Translation and Narrative Technique in MT 8:1–17, LXX 8:1–17, and AT 7:14–41.* Translated by Brian Doyle. Septuagint and Cognate Studies Series 48. Atlanta: Society of Biblical Literature, 2000.

————. "Once More, the So-Called Esther Fragments of Cave 4." *Revue de Qumran* 75 (2000) 401–21.

————. *Rewriting the Sacred Text: What the Old Greek Texts Tell Us about the Literary Growth of the Bible.* Text-Critical Studies. Atlanta: Society of Biblical Literature, 2003.

De Troyer, Kristin, and Leah Rediger Schulte. "Is God Absent or Present in the Book of Esther? An Old Problem Revisited." In *The Presence and Absence of God: Claremont Studies in the Philosophy of Religion, Conference 2008,* edited by Ingolf U. Dalferth, 35–40. Religion in Philosophy and Theology 42; Tübingen, Germany: Mohr Siebeck, 2009.

Demaray, C. E. "Esther." Chapter 9 in *Beacon Bible Commentary,* vol. 2, edited by A. F. Harper. Kansas City, MO: Beacon Hill, 1969.

Dorsett, Lyle W., and Marjorie Lamp Mead, eds. *C. S. Lewis Letters to Children.* New York: Collins, 1985.

Driscoll, Mark. *Esther.* Sermon series. 11 parts: http://marshill.com/media/esther.

Duguid, Iain M. *Esther and Ruth.* Reformed Expository Commentary. Philipsburg, NJ: P. & R., 2005.

Dunne, John Anthony. "Cast Out the Aggressive Agitators (Gl 4:29–30): Suffering, Identity, and the Ethics of Expulsion in Paul's Mission to the Galatians." In *Sensitivity to Outsiders,* edited by Jacobus Kok et al. Tübingen, Germany: Mohr Siebeck, forthcoming 2014.

————. "Suffering and Covenantal Hope in Galatians: A Critique of the 'Apocalyptic Reading' and Its Proponents." *Scottish Journal of Theology* (forthcoming).

————. "Suffering in Vain: A Study of the Interpretation of ΠΑΣΧΩ in Galatians 3.4." *Journal for the Study of the New Testament* 36 (2013) 3–16.

Edwards, Bruce. *Further Up & Further In: Understanding C. S. Lewis's The Lion, the Witch and the Wardrobe.* Nashville: Broadman & Holman, 2005.

Eissfeldt, Otto. *Old Testament: An Introduction.* Translated by Peter Ackroyd. New York: Harper & Row, 1965.

Esther and the King. DVD. Directed by Raoul Walsh and Mario Bava. Los Angeles: Twentieth Century Fox, 1960.

Esther and the King: Musical Adventures in Faith. DVD. Directed by Aaron Edson and Dennis Agle Jr. Provo, UT: Lightstone, 2010.

Exile: Esther. DVD. Directed by Amos Gitai. Chicago: Facets, 1986.

Firth, David G. *The Message of Esther: God Present but Unseen.* Bible Speaks Today. Downers Grove, IL: InterVarsity, 2010.

Fox, Michael V. *Character and Ideology in the Book of Esther.* Grand Rapids: Eerdmans, 2001.

————. *The Redaction of the Books of Esther: On Reading Composite Texts.* Society of Biblical Literature Monograph Series 40. Atlanta: Scholars, 1991.

Fuerst, Wesley J. *The Books of Ruth, Esther, Ecclesiastes, the Song of Songs, Lamentations.* Cambridge: Cambridge University Press, 1975.

Gesenius, Wilhelm. *Hebrew Grammar.* 2nd English ed. Edited by E. Kautzsch. Oxford: Clarendon, 1956.

Goldingay, John. *Ezra, Nehemiah, and Esther for Everyone.* Old Testament for Everyone. Louisville: Westminster John Knox, 2012.

Gordis, Robert. "Studies in the Esther Narrative." *Journal of Biblical Literature* 95 (1976) 43–58.

Goswell, Greg. "The Order of the Books in the Greek Old Testament." *Journal of the Evangelical Theological Society* 52 (2009) 449–66.

————. "The Order of the Books in the Hebrew Bible." *Journal of the Evangelical Theological Society* 51 (2008) 673–88.

————. "The Order of the Books in the New Testament." *Journal of the Evangelical Theological Society* 53 (2010) 225–41.

The Greatest Adventure: Stories from the Bible; Queen Esther. VHS. Directed by Don Lusk and Ray Patterson. Los Angeles: Hanna-Barbera, 1992.

Grossfeld, Bernard. *The Two Targums of Esther: Translated, with Apparatus and Notes.* The Aramaic Bible 18. Edinburgh: T. & T. Clark, 1991.

Grudem, Wayne A. *Systematic Theology: An Introduction to Biblical Doctrine.* Grand Rapids: Zondervan, 2004.

Hallo, William W., and K. Lawson Younger. *The Context of Scripture.* 3 vols. Leiden: Brill, 1997–2003.

Hamilton, James M., Jr. *God's Glory in Salvation through Judgment: A Biblical Theology.* Wheaton, IL: Crossway, 2010.

Hanhart, Robert. *Esther.* 2nd ed. Septuaginta, Vetus Testamentum Graecum 8.3. Göttingen, Germany: Vandenhoeck & Ruprecht, 1983.

Harrington, Daniel J. *Invitation to the Apocrypha.* Grand Rapids: Eerdmans, 1999.

Hays, Christopher M., and Christopher B. Ansberry. *Evangelical Faith and the Challenge of Historical Criticism.* London: SPCK, 2013.

Herodotus. *The Histories.* Translated by Aubrey de Sélincourt. Rev. ed. London: Penguin, 2003.

Holmes, Michael W. *The Apostolic Fathers.* 2nd ed. Translated by J. B. Lightfoot and J. R. Harmer. Grand Rapids: Baker, 1989.

Huey, F. B., Jr. "Esther." In *The Expositor's Bible Commentary,* edited by Frank Gaebelein and Richard P. Polcyn, 4:775–839. Grand Rapids: Zondervan, 1988.

————. "Irony as the Key to Understanding the Book of Esther." *Southwestern Journal of Theology* 32 (1990) 36–39.

Humphreys, W. Lee. "A Life-Style for Diaspora: A Study of the Tales of Esther and Daniel." *Journal of Biblical Literature* 92 (1973) 211–23.

Jobes, Karen H. *The Alpha-Text of Esther: Its Character and Relationship to the Masoretic Text.* Society of Biblical Literature Dissertation Series 153. Atlanta: Scholars, 1996.

———. *Esther.* NIV Application Commentary. Grand Rapids: Zondervan, 1999.

Jobes, Karen H., and Moisés Silva. *Invitation to the Septuagint.* Grand Rapids: Baker, 2000.

Josephus, Flavius. *Josephus: The Complete Works.* Translated by William Whiston. Nashville: Thomas Nelson, 1998.

Joüon, Paul. *A Grammar of Biblical Hebrew.* 2nd ed. Translated by Takamitsu Muraoka. Subsidia Biblica 27. Rome: Gregorian & Biblical, 2009.

Kaiser, Walt. *Recovering the Unity of the Bible: One Continuous Story, Plan, and Purpose.* Grand Rapids: Zondervan, 2009.

Keil, Carl Friedrich, and Franz Delitzsch. *Commentary on the Old Testament in Ten Volumes.* Vol. 3, *I & II Kings, I & II Chronicles, Ezra, Nehemiah, Esther.* Grand Rapids: Eerdmans, 1983.

Klaassen, Matthew J. "Persian/Jew/Jew/Persian: Levels of Irony in the Scroll of Esther." *Direction* 25 (1996) 21–28.

Kuyper, Abraham. *Women of the Old Testament: 50 Devotional Messages for Women's Groups.* Grand Rapids: Zondervan, 1979.

Laffey, Alice L. *Wives, Harlots and Concubines: The Old Testament in Feminist Perspective.* London: SPCK, 1990.

Laniak, Timothy S. *Shame and Honor in the Book of Esther.* Society of Biblical Literature Dissertation Series 165. Atlanta: Scholars, 1998.

Larson, Knute, and Kathy Dahlen. *Ezra, Nehemiah, Esther.* Holman Old Testament Commentary 9. Nashville: Broadman & Holman, 2005.

Law, Timothy Michael. *When God Spoke Greek: The Septuagint and the Making of the Christian Bible.* Oxford: Oxford University Press, 2013.

Levenson, Jon D. *Esther: A Commentary.* London: SCM, 1997.

Lewis, C. S. *The Chronicles of Narnia.* New York: HarperCollins, 2001.

———. *The Collected Letters of C. S. Lewis.* Vol. 3, *Narnia, Cambridge, and Joy: 1950–1963.* New York: HarperOne, 2007.

———. "On Stories." In *C. S. Lewis: Essay Collection & Other Short Pieces,* edited by Lesley Walmsley, 83–96. London: HarperCollins, 2000.

———. *Prayer: Letters to Malcolm.* In *C. S. Lewis: Selected Books.* London: HarperCollins, 2011.

Lofts, Norah. *Esther.* Birmingham, UK: Tree of Life, 2005.

Longenecker, Richard N. *Galatians.* Word Biblical Commentary 41. Dallas: Word, 1990.

The Lord of the Rings. Trilogy. DVD. Directed by Peter Jackson. Los Angeles: New Line, 2001–2003.

Luther, Martin. *The Table Talk of Martin Luther.* Translated by William Hazlitt. Philadelphia: United Lutheran Publication House, 1904.

Magness, Jodi. *The Archaeology of Qumran and the Dead Sea Scrolls.* Grand Rapids: Eerdmans, 2002.

Martin, John B. "Esther." In Walvoord and Zuck, *Bible Knowledge Commentary: An Exposition of the Scriptures,* edited by John F. Walvoord and Roy B. Zuck, 699–714. Wheaton, IL: Victor Books, 1986.

Martin, R. A. "Syntax Criticism of the LXX Additions to the Book of Esther." *Journal of Biblical Literature* 94 (1975) 65–72.

McClure, Albert L. "Esther's Banquet for Haman: Esther 5:4." Unpublished paper presented at the Rocky Mountain-Great Plains Regional Meeting of AAR/SBL/ASOR, Denver Seminary, April 6, 2013.

McConville, J. G. *Ezra, Nehemiah, and Esther.* Daily Study Bible. Philadelphia: Westminster, 1985.

McGee, J. Vernon. *Ruth and Esther: Women of Faith.* Nashville: Thomas Nelson, 1988.

———. *Thru the Bible with J. Vernon McGee.* Vol. 2, *Joshua–Psalms.* Pasadena, CA: Thru the Bible Radio, 1983.

Milik, J. T. *Ten Years of Discovery in the Wilderness of Judaea.* Studies in Biblical Theology 26. London: SCM, 1959.

Moore, Carey A. *Daniel, Esther, and Jeremiah: The Additions.* The Anchor Bible. Garden City, NY: Doubleday, 1977.

———. *Esther: Introduction, Translation, and Notes.* The Anchor Bible 7b. Garden City, NY: Doubleday, 1971.

———. "On the Origins of the LXX Additions to the Book of Esther." *Journal of Biblical Literature* 92 (1973) 382–93.

Moore, Beth. *Esther: It's Tough Being a Woman.* Nashville: LifeWay, 2009.

Moore, Heather B. *Esther the Queen.* American Fork, UT: Covenant Communications, 2013.

One Night with the King. DVD. Directed by Michael O. Sajbel. Hollywood: Gener8Xion, 2006.

Oz the Great and Powerful. DVD. Directed by Sam Raimi. Burbank, CA: Disney, 2013.

Pannenberg, Wolfhart. *Systematic Theology.* 3 vols. Translated by Geoffrey W. Bromiley. Grand Rapids: Eerdmans, 2010.

Paton, Lewis Bayles. *A Critical and Exegetical Commentary on the Book of Esther.* International Critical Commentary. Edinburgh: T. & T. Clark, 1908.

Pfeiffer, Charles F. *The Wycliffe Bible Commentary.* Chicago: Moody, 1962.

Pierce, Ronald W. "The Politics of Esther and Mordecai: Courage or Compromise?" *Bulletin for Biblical Research* 2 (1992) 75–89.

Piper, John. *Esther.* Wheaton, IL: Crossway, 2012.

Reid, Debra. *Esther.* Tyndale Old Testament Commentaries 13. Downers Grove, IL: InterVarsity, 2008.

Ryken, Leland. *Words of Delight: A Literary Introduction to the Bible.* Grand Rapids: Baker, 1987.

Schultz, Friedrich Wilhelm. "The Book of Esther." In *Commentary on the Holy Scriptures,* by Johann Peter Lange, translated and edited by James Strong, volume 4. Grand Rapids: Zondervan, 1960.

Semenye, Lois. "Esther." In *Africa Bible Commentary: A One-Volume Commentary Written by 70 African Scholars,* edited by Tokunboh Adeyemo, 559–68. 2nd ed. Grand Rapids: Zondervan, 2010.

Smith, Gary V. *Ezra, Nehemiah, Esther.* Cornerstone Biblical Commentary. Carol Stream, IL: Tyndale, 2010.

Star Wars. DVD. Directed by George Lucas et al. San Francisco: Lucasfilm, 1977–2005.

Starling, David I. *Not My People: Gentiles as Exiles in Pauline Hermeneutics.* Berlin: de Gruyter, 2011.

Swindoll, Charles R. *Esther: A Woman of Strength & Dignity.* Profiles in Character. Nashville: Thomas Nelson, 1997.

Talmon, Shemaryahu. "'Wisdom' in the Book of Esther." *Vetus Testamentum* 13 (1963) 419–55.

Taussig, Hal. *A New New Testament: A Bible for the 21st Century Combining Traditional and Newly Discovered Texts.* New York: Houghton Mifflin Harcourt, 2013.

Tomasino, Anthony. "Esther." In *Zondervan Illustrated Bible Background Commentary,* edited by John Walton, 3:468–505. Grand Rapids: Zondervan, 2009.

VanderKam, James C. *The Dead Sea Scrolls Today.* 2nd ed. Grand Rapids: Eerdmans, 2010.

VanderKam, James C., and Peter Flint. *The Meaning of the Dead Sea Scrolls: Their Significance for Understanding the Bible, Judaism, Jesus, and Christianity.* New York: HarperOne, 2004.

Vaux, Roland de. *Archaeology and the Dead Sea Scrolls.* London: Oxford University, 1973.

Veggie Tales: Esther, the Girl Who Became Queen. DVD. Directed by Mike Nawrocki. Nashville: Big Idea, 2003.

Vermes, Geza. *The Complete Dead Sea Scrolls in English.* Penguin Classics. Rev. Ed. London: Penguin, 2004.

Vos, Howard F. *Ezra, Nehemiah, and Esther.* Bible Study Commentary Series. Grand Rapids: Zondervan, 1987.

Walfish, Barry. *Esther in Medieval Garb: Jewish Interpretation of the Book of Esther in the Middle Ages.* Albany: State University of New York Press, 1993.

Waltke, Bruce K., and M. O'Connor. *An Introduction to Biblical Hebrew Syntax.* Winona Lake, IN: Eisenbrauns, 1990.

Waltke, Bruce K., and Charles Yu. *An Old Testament Theology: An Exegetical, Canonical, and Thematic Approach.* Grand Rapids: Zondervan, 2007.

Ward, Michael. *Planet Narnia: The Seven Heavens in the Imagination of C. S. Lewis.* Oxford: Oxford University Press, 2010.

Webb, Barry G. *Five Festal Garments: Christian Reflections on the Song of Songs, Ruth, Lamentations, Ecclesiastes, Esther.* Downers Grove, IL: InterVarsity, 2000.

Wells, Samuel, and George Sumner. *Esther & Daniel.* Brazos Theological Commentary on the Bible. Grand Rapids: Brazos, 2013.

Wicked: The Untold Story of the Witches of Oz. Play. Written by Stephen Schwartz. Directed by Joe Mantello. Hollywood: Pantages, 2007–2009.

Wiebe, John M. "Esther 4:14: 'Will Relief and Deliverance Arise for the Jews from Another Place?'" *Catholic Biblical Quarterly* 53 (1991) 409–15.

The Wizard of Oz. DVD. Directed by Victor Fleming et al. Burbank, CA: Warner Bros., 1939.

Wolf, Joan. *A Reluctant Queen: The Love Story of Esther.* Nashville: Thomas Nelson, 2011.

Wolfe, Lisa M. *Ruth, Esther, Song of Songs, and Judith.* Eugene, OR: Cascade, 2011.

Wright, N. T. *Jesus and the Victory of God.* Christian Origins and the Question of God 2. Minneapolis: Fortress, 1996.

Yamauchi, Edwin M. *Persia and the Bible.* Grand Rapids: Baker, 1996.

Ancient Document Index

~

APOCRYPHA

~

Pseudepigrapha

~

New Testament

~

DEAD SEA SCROLLS

~

RABBINIC WRITINGS

Name Index

Allen, L. C., 23, 33
Anderson, B. W., 17, 64, 97, 111
Anderson, G. A., 50
Andrews, G., 2, 24, 57, 85, 87, 124–25
Ansberry, C. B., 106

Bakri, M., 63
Baldwin, J. G., 16, 43, 48–49, 60, 62, 70, 77
Barnes, A., 36
Barth, K., 102
Bechtel, C. M., 32, 64
Beckett, M., 114, 120–21
Beckwith, R. T., 99–100
Berkhof, L., 102
Berlin A., 1, 6, 29, 31, 36, 42, 48, 59, 61–62, 78, 99–100, 112, 119
Berg, S. B., 59, 114, 116
Bickerman, E. J., 23
Bjornard, R. B., 36, 48
Blomberg, C., 104
Breneman, M., 36, 43–44, 46, 50, 100
Brettler, M. Z., 42
Brown, D., 107–8
Bush, F. W., 31, 46, 48, 54, 59, 61–62, 97–98, 134

Calvin, J., 102
Carruthers, J., 18, 82
Childs, B. S., 65, 96, 109
Clark, E., 53

Clines, D. J. A., 44, 60–61, 68, 70, 115, 132, 134–35
Conti, M., 97
Craig, K. M., 60
Crawford, S. A. W., 66

Dahlen, K., 32, 48
Day, L., 47
De Troyer, K., 60–61, 97, 99, 132–34
Delitzsch, F., 36
Demaray, C. E., 48
Dorsett, L. W., 122
Driscoll, M., 41–42
Duguid, I. M., 57
Dunne, J. A., xi, 71

Edwards, B., 122
Eissfeldt, O., 98

Firth, D. G., 31–32, 39, 46, 60, 66, 117
Flint, P., 99
Fox, M. V., 5, 6, 23–25, 30–32, 36, 43, 46, 54, 61–62, 64, 69, 99, 114, 118, 132–34, 136
Fuerst, W. J., 32, 60

Gesenius, W., 46
Gitai, A., 63
Goldingay, J., 6, 28, 32, 36, 43
Goswell, G., 123
Gordis, R., 62
Grossfeld, B., 78

Subject Index

CPSIA information can be obtained
at www.ICGtesting.com
Printed in the USA
FSHW011738080920
73628FS

9 781620 327845